Harley-Davidson Twin Cam
Hop-Up & Rebuild Manual
Build a Twin Cam that's Fast *and* Durable

Timothy Remus
with
R&R Cycles

Published by:
Wolfgang Publications Inc.
P.O. Box 223
Stillwater, MN 55082
www.wolfpub.com

Legals

First published in 2017 by Wolfgang Publications Inc.,
P.O. Box 223, Stillwater MN 55082

ISBN: 978-1-929133-69-7

Harley-Davidson Twin Cam, Hop-Up & Rebuild Manual

From the Publisher

Every book starts as an idea. When I decided to do a Twin Cam engine book, I also decided I needed a partner: a well known shop where I could take photos of the various assembly sequences, a shop with a staff who could help with the technical information. A shop with a well respected name so the book would be respected in the marketplace.

Among all the builders and customerizers I've met over the last 20-plus years, there is one who truly knows everyone who's anyone in the custom Harley world. Thus, when I started looking for a partner to help me with a Twin Cam Hop-up and Building book, I asked David Perewitz for help. With his typical enthusiasm, Dave said only two words: "R&R Cycles." After a short pause he went on to explain why they were the perfect shop to help me with a serious engine-building book.

David explained first that they built the motor that took daughter Jody Perewitz to a series of records on the Bonneville Salt Flats. Second, they've been a major player in the high-performance engine business in the Northeast for years and years. Third, they're a shop that isn't afraid to step up and buy the tools and talent to do the job right. "When they couldn't buy enough transmission main shafts from the aftermarket to keep up with production," explained David, "they went out and bought a new CNC just to cut those shafts."

R&R stands for Reggie and Reggie Jr. It was Reggie Jr., who answered the phone when I called to introduce myself. It took only a few minutes before he "got it." We were on the same page as they say. And when I called again a day or two later, Reggie Jr. and I were able to agree in principle to be partners in a Twin Cam book, the one you hold in your hands.

Making a deal over the phone is one thing, making all the promises of cooperation and friendship come true is another thing all together. So it was with caution that I scheduled a short visit just to test the waters. Partly because not all mechanics or crews welcome interlopers equipped with cameras and computers into their own private world.

In the case of R&R, I needn't have worried. From Brandon in the shop to Pete at the counter and Tim in the machine shop, everyone seemed genuinely pleased to see me there and happy to cooperate in any way they could. My second trip went as well as the first. And when I called R&R, after returning home, to help me by taking some photos for that I missed, they were happy to comply.

David was right when he said R&R was the perfect shop to help with an engine-building book. From the shop in front to the unit-assembly room in back, the crew at R&R are nothing but professional. Equipped with the best tools and equipment (some of it of their design), there really isn't much they can't do when it comes to building and modifying V-Twin engines.

I feel honored and lucky to have access to the shop and crew at R&R. And I'm proud to call them my partner in the production of this Twin Cam Engine Hop-Up and Building book.

Introduction

What it is - What it's not

Yes, this is a book about V-Twin, Twin Cam engines. No, it's not a book about deciding which camshafts to use, or which throttle body will make the most power.

Really, this is an engine book that focuses on the engine building - period.

Readers will find a lot of information on porting, and on the design of ports and heads. All of which relates to making good power. But, the information comes through as part of the building process.

Some of the procedures shown here are not applicable to a home based (or small shop) engine-building operation. Yet, it's good information. And when you do take the crank in for welding, truing and balancing, you will know what questions to ask, and what you're getting for your money.

I always think of a performance engine as a piece of jewelry. And I think that parallel is brought out in this book. The guys at R&R don't just assemble engines or fix Harleys. They take it to the next level. When Chris does a porting job, he wants to know how the owner rides the bike and which cams they plan to run. When Jon assembles one of R&R's 124 inch Twin Cam motors, he wants to know if it's destined to be a street engine, or a race engine - as the clearances are slightly different from one to the other.

Speaking of the R&R staff, the book contains a number of interviews with members of the crew. I think it's a good way to let the people with the knowledge share that knowledge with readers. You'll learn a few things that aren't in any of the books, all the little details that only someone with twenty or thirty years of building engines knows. Sometimes, a skilled tech will pass along a gem of information almost as an afterthought during an interview.

The idea was, and is, to provide detailed building and assembling sequences that show how to build it right. Whether you're doing a top end on an engine that's still in the chassis, or assembling a true kick-ass big block on the bench, the sequence is here. Along with related information on things like crank truing, welding and balancing.

All the procedures are explained in detail. Abundant photos make it easier to understand. And captions approved by the technicians and experts helps to ensure you get maximum usefulness from each photo or illustration.

Ultimately it's about having the correct technical information, combined with the right attitude. As shown in the R&R shop, you can never overstate the importance of precision, cleanliness, and being very, very thorough.

Chapter One

R&R Cycles

Born in the Basement

Located in the small city of Manchester, NH, R&R Cycles, started in the early '90s as a part-time, home-based polishing operation. What started in the basement of his parent's house by the younger of the two Rs, is currently a first class service and hop-up shop for American V-Twins.

Walking through the front door of R&R can be a bit deceiving. Like many aftermarket "Harley shops" this one has a small showroom ringed by a group of used bikes sporting For Sale tags.

R&R is known for many things, including complete big-inch V-twins in both Evo and Twin Cam configurations, and a variety of top-end kits available in variations from mild to wild.

Everything from very nice late model Baggers, to Bourget pro street bikes dating to the early two-thousands when the after-market bikes were king of the hill.

Walk a little farther into the showroom and there's a parts counter, backed by pegboard, and to your left, another shorter counter with a glass top and a cash register on one end.

Continue past the counters and you will find the shop, complete with 6 or 8 Handy Lifts each occupied by a bike in the shop for service and repair. Behind the ten or twelve bikes in the shop for service wait four times that many two-wheeled machines waiting their turn on one of the hoists. If you make a turn to the left at the back of the shop you find the proverbial well-equipped dyno room.

All of this seems normal enough, a busy, well-kept service and repair facility, filled with disassembled Softails, Baggers and Customs. We've all see similar shops on many occasions. It's when you walk past the shop, and through the bikes waiting for service, that you begin to realize that R&R isn't just one more pretty face.

Walk through a doorway and you find what is essentially a whole 'nother building - the other half of R&R.

What you find starts with an engine assembly

From the front showroom, R&R Cycles looks like any small to medium size aftermarket V-Twin shop, but the deeper you dig the more there is to see.

Reggie Jr. wears a lot of hats at R&R - primary among them is Service Manager.

The shop stays busy all year long, with the normal super-busy spring rush that most shops experience. Though the work runs the gamut from tires to brakes, the biggest single category is engine repair and hop up.

Though R&R doesn't build as many motors from scratch as they did in the industry's heyday, there are alway three to five engines being assembled at any given time.

area complete with a multitude of engines in mid-assembly, along with the various fixtures and specialized tools needed to do the job right.

On the far end of the room is a dynamic balancer for V-Twin cranks, and a drill press for removing material from the flywheels. Past the assembly room things really get interesting. On one side there's the valve grinding machine, a manual lathe and a sophisticated cylinder honing machine.

What really dominates the room however, are the CNC machines. There are fresh head castings in one machine getting their ports opened up, piston pins and flywheel shafts on another, and raw cylinder assemblies on the third.

The CNC machines came into the shop in the days that R&R was selling well over 200 complete engines to companies like Bourget, Confederate and all the rest. They were purchased as a way to keep up with all that demand. They were also purchased simply because at R&R they like to have complete control of their products, from beginning to end.

Many of the components that make up an R&R engine start out as castings or forgings manufactured from materials and to specifications specified by R&R. Flywheel components start as forgings, made from 4340 steel and then shipped to R&R.

Once in the shop, Tim takes over. First carving the raw 'wheels into a recognizable shape, before boring the holes for the piston pin and then the pinion and sprocket shafts.

From the engine assembly room to the cutting done on the various CNC machines, a certain obsession with accuracy pervades the shop. Jon, in the assembly room, washes everything at least three times before mating one component to another. Chris, the resident porting expert, explains how you can't have even a spec of dust on the valve seats before installing them into the head. In the end, most of the components machined or assembled in the back room are held to accuracy that's plus or minus just a few ten-thousandths of an inch.

It's their obsession with accuracy, combined with a related insistence that all components be manufactured from the best materials available, that makes R&R components among the best available from the aftermarket.

Two shops in one, R&R Cycles is a great place to take your Bagger or your Softail for just a little more power - it's also a manufacturer of everything from cylinder heads to complete engines with displacements that reach all the way to 155 cubic inches. And yes, there are parts for Indians in the pipeline.

What separates R&R from the more typical aftermarket shop is the manufacturing that goes on in the "back room." Their crank assemblies are a good example: everything from the pinion shaft...

.... to the flywheel halves are machined in house from blanks manufactured to R&R specs.

9

Q&A, Reggie Jr.

Reggie Jr. The man who started it all in Dad's basement and remains responsible for most day to day decisions at R&R.

In the case of components like cylinder heads, the casting is done by an outside firm, though all the finish and porting work is done in-house.

Reggie, let's start with your history and the history of R&R?

I started polishing parts in my Father's basement, that's where it all started. That was late '91 or early '92. He had an old lathe in the basement and I used that. I started customizing my bike, taking parts off and polishing them. My friends liked what I was doing and asked me to polish their parts. One thing led to another and we were rebuilding engines less than two years later. Of course, we needed more equipment if we were going to do serious engine work.

In '92 we added milling machines and a Superflow bench in the basement. And pretty soon we had three dynos in my parent's thee-car garage; one set up for tuning, one for racing, and one for development work. We also worked with some software developers to test and de-bug their engine software.

Needless to say, the business really took over Mom and Dad's house.

So, what happened next?

We realized we liked the business enough to try and do it for a living - we started looking for a building. I think my Mom was happy to get us out of the house. No more baking parts in her oven. We moved into the building we're in now in April of '95.

Then how did you progress once you moved into the new building?

Well, we started out in the middle of the building, where our service department is now. There was an automotive repair facility in the building when we bought it and they stayed in the building for about seven years. We just kind of grew around their operation and took over other parts of the building. In 2008 we added on to the building. Just as the economy and the custom bike business both crashed.

I remember we moved in September of '08. We had just received our occupancy permit, we were making the first payments on the new mortgage - which was a lot bigger than it was before - and the phone stopped ringing. It sucked.

We realized then that motorcycle parts were not the only thing that the machine shop could make. The custom industry was slowly dying and that's where we'd put most of our eggs. So we found some outside, non-motorcycle, work to do. That way we could continue doing the bike work. The other work, it was making aircraft parts, grew and subsidized the motorcycle operation.

But let's backup, before the crash and before the expanded building, you were doing a lot of work for the big aftermarket companies?

We did a lot with Bourget, I was selling 35 to 50 Bourgets per year, and we were selling them engines. We manufactured a lot of engines. Confederate was buying 200 of our engines per

Even CNCs don't truely run themselves. Here long-time machinist Tim, on the left, discusses the accuracy of the cuts done to a flywheel, with Reggie Sr.

Heads of their own design are a big item at R&R, and there's always a rack or two of heads waiting for porting and final assembly.

The slower winter season leaves time to build up an inventory of R&R parts in preparation for the spring rush.

year, and the Chopper builders were buying them too. We couldn't build them fast enough. And then just like that, everything changed.

Can you talk about what R&R is now, i.e. where does your business come from now?

Now we are more diversified, not all our eggs are in one basket. Not only do we have outside, non-motorcycle contracts, but the motorcycle business itself is more diverse. We don't build parts for just Harley-Davidsons anymore. We've started to add Indian and Polaris parts to our catalog.

And we're doing more service, that's going really well. Since the crash a lot of people have given up their choppers, but that doesn't mean they stopped riding. Some bought Baggers and bring them to us for service and upgrades. We picked up a lot of new customers that way.

The other good thing we've done is add storage. We have an upper level filled with storage bikes. It's been good for our business, 70% of the people who bring their bikes in for storage have something done while it's here.

You work the front end of the shop a lot. How do you advise a customer who comes in with a desire to "go faster" or "have more power"?

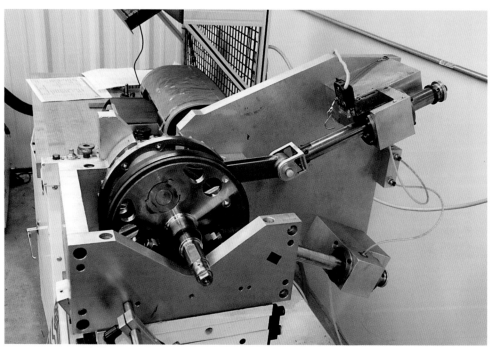

Another example of the lengths that R&R will go to in order to get the parts they think are good enough - R&R bought a new dynamic balancer, then modified the support system and wrote their own software - before putting it into service.

I try and give them the most honest and reliable answer I can. Some who come in are searching for answers, and some who come in think they know it all. Sometimes it takes kid gloves. I want to help them out and I don't want to insult anyone. I walk them through the shop so they can get a visual and understand what we do. I try to explain our shop and how we do it differently than someone else might.

Truing is a multi-step process done in the engine assembly room. Note the dynamic balancer in the background.

Do you sometimes have to tell them not to do something, do you have to turn down work occasionally if what they want to do is a bad idea?

Yes, sometimes. I don't like using customers for Guinea Pigs. I also don't want to rely on someone else's parts that I'm afraid might fail, or not give the customer good longevity. Yes, I will turn down work.

We also get situations where maybe they have a tuner already, and they want one of our stage 4 kits, but we have to tell them the tuner won't work with the stage 4, it won't let us take it far enough. We have to tell them they either buy another tuner or we can't install the package.

Exhaust systems are another big thing.

A lot of crank assemblies - from a variety of manufacturers - get welded, trued and balanced at R&R.

Cylinders for the 124 inch R&R engine are final-machined in-house, mated to pistons manufactured to a R&R design.

They spent the money, and it's hard to tell them they have to spend it twice. But we can't tell them they're going to have a hundred horses from the engine kit we install when in reality they will only get 70 with the pipes currently on the bike.

When they come in, I talk with them, it's almost like an interview. You have to find out what are they're really looking for, what do they want for the end result. How much do they want to spend? The two don't always coincide.

I don't want to sell something they aren't going to be happy with, I want them happy the first time. I don't want them to come back and say, "this wasn't exactly what I was looking for." Sometimes I tell them to wait another year so they will know what they really want. I think that's helped us, that honesty. But I've also had customers go to other shops.

Tell me about kits, why are kits a good idea?

They are made up of parts that we know will work together, there's no experimenting. We aren't just putting in a collection of parts that may or may not work

Chris, resident cylinder head expert, does all the hand porting on every head that comes through the shop - from R&R's own 124 heads to Harley heads that are part of Stage 2 to 4 kits.

well together - there are no surprises.

Give me a breakdown of the kits you have for Twin Cams?

We have 4 top end kits. And 3 kits that get into building the lower end of the engine, the 117, 120, 124 inch kits.

So it comes down to how much power do you want and how much money do you want to spend?

Yes, Stage 2 is a fairly mild package. It uses mild compression, and mild cams. Stage 2 is great for touring. Lots of torque down low, but doesn't build the horsepower up at a high RPM. Our kits go all the way to stage 5. That's a 103 inch, 120 horse engine. That's a lot of motor for a 103. And they still make nice drivable power at the lower end, A lot of that streetability is made possible by fuel injection. You don't have to rely on a carb that was chosen to make that big power, but will give you shitty results down low.

When riders or shops hop up the motor and get

a poor result, what are the typical mistakes they commonly make?

They usually over cam and under compression. Essentially what they have is not a good combination. Cams, compression and head work all go hand in hand.

So we come back to the idea of kits?

Yes, you get a known result, you're not guessing about the results, it's proven. That package will give you the results you are looking for. You can look through the magazines and one says a certain part will give you a ten percent improvement and another says a twenty percent improvement. You can put all those parts in your bike and still get a poor result, not because they're bad parts, but because those parts are not meant to work together.

And with R&R kits, most of the parts are your own? And they've been tested together?

Most of our parts, if we don't actually manu-

Monster motors are no stranger at R&R. shown are cylinders for 127, 140 and 143 cubic inch engines, manufactured from both aluminum and steel.

A lot of flywheels come into R&R, and some of them leave in the metal-recycle truck.

Like almost everything else at R&R, welding cranks so they don't shift - ever - is done in-house.

facture them, we design them and have them made to our specifications. Like pistons for example, our pistons are our design - for things like piston pin location, deck height, ring locations, type of rings being used, the shape of the dome.

I see a lot of failed cranks in the back of the shop. Are cranks a big deal these days?

Yes, cranks are a big thing. If you feel unusual vibration, stop and have it checked, don't just continue. The way the bearings are set up now with no Timken bearings, once the cranks do go out (meaning one or both of the individual flywheels move slightly on the common crankpin and become out of phase), they will start to hurt those roller bearings. They rip the side-walls right out of the bearings, then the pieces of metal that were the side-walls start to run through the engine, where they get caught in the oil pump or block an oil passage. I've even seen the rollers come right out of the bearing assembly. That's why we like to weld the cranks.

Is it consistent, are all the riders who ride hard having issues with their cranks?

No, it's more hit and miss. I've seen cranks that are out of spec from the factory. And I've seen cranks with 40K on the clock, from engines putting out 110 horsepower, and those are not out at all.

Every time we do a performance package the first thing we do is a check for crank run out. If it's good we build the engine. If it's out, we call the customer and explain that we can put it back together stock, or we can rebuild the crank. Even if runout is only moderate (between good and bad) we call the customer and give them options. We don't want the customer to have any surprises.

The tooling used to press together the flywheel assemblies was designed and manufactured in-house.

There are no newbies - the current crew is made up of long-term employees, each of whom came to R&R with extensive experience gained at outside shops

Chapter Two

Twin Cam History

The Evolution of a Design

Harley-Davidson introduced the Twin Cam engine in 1999. The first models to utilize the Twin Cam engines were the FXD (Dyna) models and the FLH (touring) models. The Softail models saw their own variation of the Twin Cam engine in 2000. This engine was named the Twin Cam "B" because it contained internal balancers. These balancers were chain driven and timed from a sprocket on the crank assembly. As with all Harley-Davidson engines of the past, each

What started as a new, 88 cubic inch V-Twin, soon grew to 96, then 103, and here, 110 cubic inches. And of course if you want more, those super-extra cubes are available from both the aftermarket and Milwaukee.

engine model is an upgrade to its predecessor and the Twin Cam was no exception. The Twin Cam engine had many fine qualities as compared to the Evo. For example: Straighter pushrod geometry due to its two-cam design, cylinders with thick walls that could be bored from 3.750 to 3.930 inches diameter for a 9 cubic inch gain, taking the engine from 88 to 97 cubic inches. Meaning large increases in displacement were achievable with only a top-end disassembly.

Like all new designs, the Twin Cam did suffer growing pains. Perhaps the worst growing pain was the spring loaded tensioners, and the short service life offered by the tensioning pads themselves.

The list of improvements included new cylinder heads with ports and combustion chambers that could be easily reworked to help this new engine make decent power from a relatively small package. The Delphi fuel injection, introduced in 2002, was leaps and bounds above carburetion, making hot rod Twin Cam engines much more user friendly.

The Twin Cam engine however, was not without its flaws. Harley-Davidson originally introduced the Twin Cam engine with spring loaded cam chain tensioners. Tensioners that could chew up the pad that rode against the chain, sometimes at low mileage figures. The debris from the worn pad would then get picked up by the oil pump, which spread the pad material throughout the engine, often damaging the oil pump and support plate in the process. Worse, some-

Here's what sometimes happened to the pads. The secondary problem was the contamination of the oil by the pad material.

The factory introduced hydraulic tensioners, no more springs, in 2006 on the Dyna models.

Both the main cam drive chain and the cam-to-cam chain, were kept in tension with oil pressure, not springs.

times the pad would completely break apart sending chunks throughout the gear chest damaging the cams, lifters and bearings. Another issue with the Twin Cam engines was the pressed together crank assemblies. Those crank assemblies would shift somewhat easily, coming out of true, causing vibration, bearing damage, support plate and oil pump damage and eventually damage to the owner's wallet.

The flaws did make for a silver lining of sorts, the aftermarket was kept busy engineering and designing products and procedures to enhance the Twin Cam engine and extend it's life. Gear drive cams would be one good example of those improvements.

Harley-Davidson had it's own ideas about shortcomings and necessary improvements to the Twin Cam. In 2006 Harley made some pretty substantial changes, Initially introduced in the Dyna line only. The changes included: internal oil passages (from engine to oil tank), a change in the engine-to-transmission bolt pattern, primary housing mounting pad and bolt pattern, the intake flange bolt pattern, larger exhaust ports and big improvements to the cams, chains, sprockets, tensioners, support plate, and oil pump. The chains and sprockets went from Harley's silent design to a standard roller style chain and sprockets. The chain tensioners were changed from spring loaded units to hydraulic assemblies, offering much longer tensioner and chain life and minimizing the likelihood that pad-debris would be spread throughout the engine.

The cam bearings were removed from the support plate leaving the cams to ride directly in the bores of the support plate itself. Oil fed directly to the cam bore creates an oil cushion for the cams to ride on. The oil pump gyrotors and support plate windows were increased in size for higher oil volume, better circulation and improved scavenging. In 2007 Harley-Davidson increased the engine displacement from 88 to 96 cubic inches and all the models received the changes that the Dyna models saw the previous year, and in 2013 the Twin Cam engine displacement became standardized at 103 cubic inches. The later engines however are not a direct replacement for the 2005 and earlier Twin Cam model bikes, they will not bolt up. The chassis dimensions have not changed however, so if you're so inclined the entire late model drivetrain will fit in the earlier chassis. Or you can take advantage of what the aftermarket has to offer for the earlier model bikes such as: cam support plates with hydraulic tensioners, higher volume oil pumps, cylinder boring and larger pistons, headwork, and all the rest.

A final note on the evolution of the Twin Cam. In the world of V-Twin motorcycles, bigger always seems better, especially when it comes to displacement. And if you can have those extra inches without disassembling the cases and messing with the flywheel, all the better. Harley-Davidson and some of the aftermarket companies have introduced big bore kits that make it possible to create a 110 cubic inch Twin Cam from a stock 103, or 117 inch engine from a stock 110. Personally, I am skeptical. I don't like the idea of using a cylinder with a spigot that has walls only .030 inches thick. They offer very little support for the piston as it goes by, and the thin lower walls mean there is no over-boring. So if a piston or cylinder is damaged you are forced to replace both the piston and the cylinder. It is a cheaper upfront cost, but I don't believe it will be cheaper in the long run.

With or without the latest 110 cube kit, as you read on I think you will find that the Twin Cam engine is certainly one of Harley-Davidson's best engines and a great foundation for just about any hot rod project.

Text by Reggie Jr.

Though the Twin Cam used in Softails, and the one used in Baggers and Dynas, look the same, only the Softail engines used chain driven balancers. Note the heat shield, an often seen accessory on Twin Cams.

Chapter Three

Top End Job - done in the Chassis

Part 1, First You Gotta Take it Apart

Whether you're doing a hop-up, or just a top end repair, there are numerous occasions when that V-Twin engine can stay in the chassis. What follows is the disassembly of a 2011 Bagger with a factory 103 engine.

The goal here is to give the owner back his bike with more displacement and a significant boost in power. First though, there's the disassembly by Brandon. And once the disassembly is done, and before the Jon can begin to truly build the "new" engine, there needs to be a careful inspection of the bottom end to ensure the new

The Twin Cam disassembly starts with a 2011 Bagger equipped with a stock 103 engine.

engine will have a solid foundation for all that extra power.

The disassembly might seem pretty straight forward, but it's always good to see how a professional does the take-down, and what kind of small-yet-important tricks he uses along the way.

The sequence starts with the seat, removal provides access to the battery so the negative cable can be disconnected. The exhaust is next, followed by the pushrods. As noted in the photos, the bolt-cutter really helps to speed things up - then it's time for the rocker covers, the cam support plate and the cams themselves.

It makes no sense to put a new top end on an engine with a questionable bottom end. One of the bottom-end issues the crew at R&R see on a regular basis is excessive runout of the pinion shaft. So, before proceeding any farther, Brandon uses a special tool from Feuling and a dial indicator to check the runout.

This particular Twin Cam has .004 inches of runout. At R&R they like to see figures of no more than .006 inches, so the disassembly continues, with the tank, followed by the rocker boxes and cylinder heads. Once the heads are off, it's relatively easy to pull the cylinders. The pistons are next, which means pulling the circlip out of the piston (note the rags stuffed in the case at this point so those little spring clips can't follow Murphy's law and land in the bottom of the cases). With the circlip safely removed from one side of piston, a special, wrist pin puller is used to pull the piston pins themselves.

Before considering the disassembly finished, it's important to check the crankshaft assembly again. Reggie checks for up and down or twist play - and any drag - at four positions on the crank pin. Obviously there should be no play, and no drag at any of those four positions.

The important point here is to determine whether of not the bottom end is in good condition. Because if it's not, then there's no point in putting a new top end on a worn out or out-of-spec bottom end.

The exhaust is one of the first things to come off - Brandon starts by removing the bolt in the support bracket as shown. An aerosol can of good penetrating oil is almost essential for bolts like this.

Next the fasteners at the heads are removed, and the exhaust can be pulled away from the left side pipe.

1. The pipes come off one at time after taking off the fasteners at the flanges, and the mounts under the bags.

2. Next on the list is removal of the spark plugs...

3. ... taking them out makes it much easier to turn the engine over - necessary for the rest of the disassembly.

4. The clips shown pop out, so the pushrod tubes can be collapsed.

5. Brandon slides the tubes up, then turns the engine over with the rear tire until he has both cams on the base circle.

1. With the cams on the base circle, Brandon uses the bolt cutter to quickly get the pushrods out of the way.

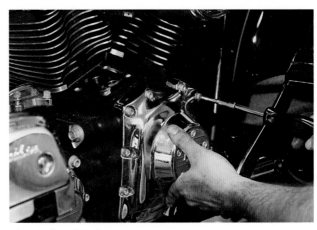

4. Under the chrome cover...

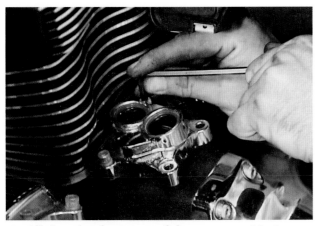

2. All 4 pushrods are out of the way, now it's time to pull the lifter blocks - Brandon recommends caution as the bolts tend to be very tight, meaning it's easy to strip out the head of the small Allen bolt.

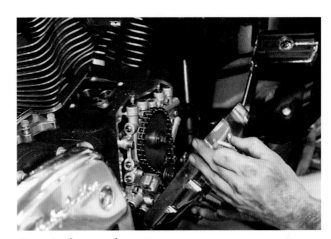

5. ...is the camchest...

3. No lifter blocks, pulling the lifters themselves is next.

6. ...and a lot of components - like this tensioner - that need to be carefully disassembled and inspected. Note, this hydraulic tensioner is used on Dynas from '06 on, and everything else from '07 on.

1. A 3/8 inch impact is used to take out, first, the cam sprocket fastener, then the pinion sprocket fasteners.

4. After pulling the 6 fasteners that hold the plate, and the 4 that hold the oil pump in place, the cam support plate can be pulled out of the camchest.

2. Next, the sprocket and chain assembly is removed.

5. The cams generally come out along with the support plate. The oil pump, however is pulled separately, after the support plate is pulled off.

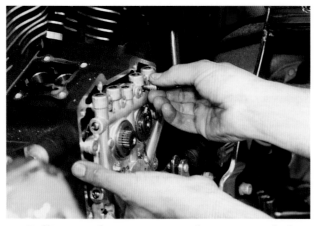

3. Pulling out the cam support plate starts with the removal of six fasteners that hold the plate in place.

6. One empty camchest. Time now to check the runout of the pinion shaft.

1. With the help of a Feuling tool and a good dial indicator, Brandon rolls the engine over and finds .004 inches of runout - which is within spec and means the disassembly can continue.

4. ... the wiring harness...

2. So off comes the tank...

5. ...and intake manifold.

3. ... followed by the air cleaner and ...

1. Rocker boxes are next, here Brandon pulls the top off the rear box.

4. Time to pull off the lower half of the rocker boxes...

2. The front motor mount comes off next.

5. ... both of which slide out of the way on the right side....

3. Here you see Brandon pulling it off the bike.

6. ... leaving a pretty bare V-Twin.

1. Each cylinder head is held on by 4 fasteners.

2. Cylinder heads lift off next...

3. ... Followed by the cylinders.

4. Once the cylinders are up and off...

5. ... it's important to stuff rags into the case bores so nothing can drop down into the cases.

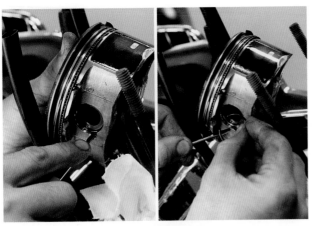

1. Brandon uses a small screw driver to pry the cir-clip out of its groove and out of the way.

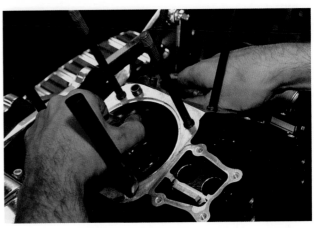

4. It's very important to check for rod play, and drag, at 4 separate positions on the crank.

2. Next, a small specialized slide-hammer is used ...

5. As Reggie Jr. explains, "there should be no up and down play, no 'twist play' and no drag, as you move the rod on the pin - in any of the 4 positions.

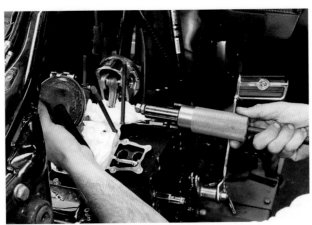

3. ...to pull each piston pin.

6. Time now to do a thorough inspection of the parts, and think about what can, and can't, be used again.

Chapter 3

Part 2
The Reassembly

Now that you're all torn down you are ready to start reassembly. For some, it's just a cam upgrade and a big bore kit, like bumping the displacement of a 96 inch engine to 103 cubic inches. On the other hand, it might be a complete top end package with new performance heads, hi compression forged pistons and aggressive cams. No matter how simple or complex the project is, the same attention to detail in reassembly is critical if you want to end up with a good running, well performing engine that will last and last.

Reassembly is more than just "the reverse of disassembly." Done correctly, assembly is done in a specific sequence, using clean parts, (often lubed before assembly) that are never forced together.

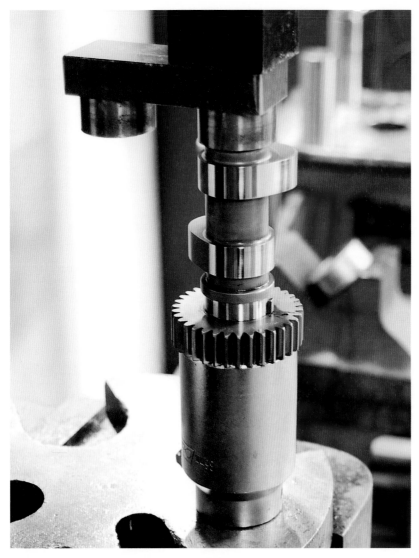

To start, Jon carefully presses camshaft in to the gear. Make sure front gear is pressed on the front cam, rear pressed onto the rear cam. Press camshaft into gear with labeling and alignment marks facing cam lobes. Press slowly and straight. DO NOT PRESS IN CROOKED.

Though it's temping to jump into the reassembly, there are a few preliminary steps that have to come first. All the parts that are going to be used again need to be inspected for wear, and before that they need to be cleaned thoroughly.

Any parts that need to go out to outside shops, like cylinders that go to the machine shop for boring, should be cleaned as well. Nobody likes to work on dirty parts. If there's any doubt about whether the cylinders you are installing have been cleaned after boring and honing, do it. Note the way the cylinders are cleaned in chapter six. At the very least, they should make a dip in the solvent tank, and then be washed with dish soap and hot water.

If all the parts are laid out on a clean bench before assembly starts, it's easy to do an inventory and make sure all the goodies are there. Nothing worse than getting halfway into a job and then be forced to stop and make a run to the local shop or dealership before you can finish up.

The sequence shows the steps Jon took in doing the reassembly at R&R.

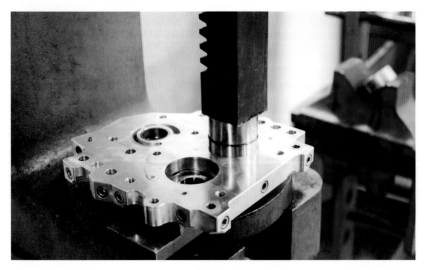

Next, the cam support bearings are pressed into place as shown.

Photos by Brandon

1. Then Jon lines up the timing marks on the cams ...

2. ... and presses them into the bearings. Don't forget to install the snap ring on the front cam where it protrudes from the support plate.

3. The cam chest ready for the installation of the support plate and cams. Note the 3 new O-rings in place to the rear of the pinion shaft. Never re-use O-rings.

4. The parts laid out prior to installation of the support plate, oil pump and drive gears.

5. The oil pump used in this case is the standard 2-stage oil pump from Harley-Davidson.

1. The inner, or suction gerotors, go in first. The inner gerotor must line up with the flat on the pinion shaft.

2. ... along with plenty of pre-lube oil.

3. The outer, or pressure gerotor, goes in last, again with a more than ample squirt of engine oil.

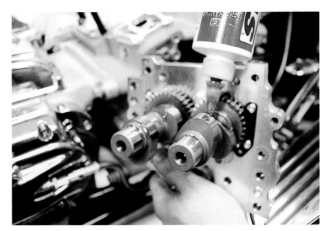

4. Now the mating gerotor is lined up and slipped into place.

5. More oil...

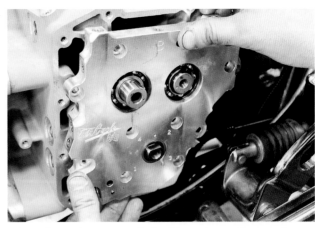

6. ... then it's time to slide the support plate and cams into place as shown.

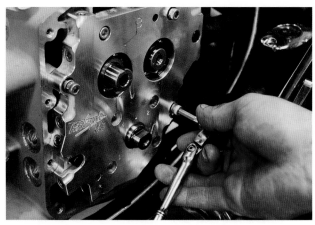

1. The R&R support plate is held in Plate with 6 Allen-head fasteners. Four of the 6 are the same length, and 2 are longer. All get a dab of blue Loctite on the threads.

2. The fasteners are final tightened in a cross pattern to 10 to 12 ft. lbs. Be sure the cams spin without any binding before moving on to the oil pump.

3. Tightening the oil pump to the support plate comes next. The 4 bolts (coated with a little blue Loctite) are hand tightened, and then with help from a second set of hands...

4. ... the 4 fasteners are tightened gradually while a helper keeps the engine turning over in a forward direction - so the oil pump components have a chance to center themselves. Final torque is 10 to 12 ft. lbs.

5. In this case the fastener is used to draw the cam gear onto the rear camshaft. Be sure to use red Loctite on the treads of both the cam bolt and the pinion bolt.

1. Slide the cam and pinion gears on to their respective shafts, be sure the two timing marks line up as shown. Before installing the fasteners, clean all the oil out of the threads in the pinion and the rear cam.

2. Apply a little red Loctite before screwing the bolts in to the crank and the rear camshaft. Be sure to chase the threads to clean off any old Loctite.

3. Torque specs for the two fasteners is 30 ft. lbs. for the upper, cam, bolt. And 20 for the lower pinion shaft fastener.

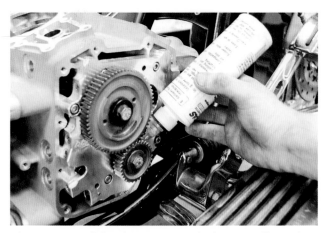

4. Be sure to lube the two gears before installing the cover.

5. Note the way the camchest cover has been "clearanced" as shown by the arrows.

6. With a new gasket in place, and some "blue" on the threads, the cover is installed and all the fasteners are tightened to 10 ft. lbs.

Chain Drive Assembly

Since the introduction of Harley-Davidson's hydraulic cam chain tensioners ('07 and up Twin Cam), chain-driven cam installation have become more common than gear-driven cams in most performance engine packages. So let's start with the typical chain drive cam setup in a late model Twin Cam. Remember to clean all your parts before hand and inspect carefully for wear or damage. Plus, reassembly is a much easier process with clean parts.

1. Insert each cam into inner cam bearings one at a time (front in front etc.). Rotate cam by hand and measure clearance between the lobe of the cam shaft and the case. You want a minimum of .030" clearance. If clearance is too tight case will have to be modified to create adequate clearance.

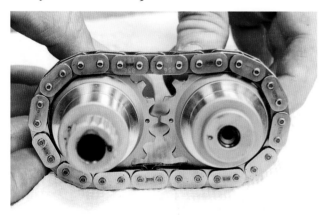

2. With either cleaned original or new inner cam chain, insert both cams. Align camshafts so the two dots on the cam sprockets line up as shown in the picture.

3. Using either clean engine oil or assembly lube, lube the bushing ends of the cam shafts and inner chain.

4. Lube cam holes in the support plate being sure to lube both the inside bore and outer face surfaces.

5. Gently slide cams into support plate from the back side. Make sure longer shaft with the toothed cog is in rear cam bore. Cams should slide in easily. DO NOT FORCE CAMS INTO PLATE.. This will damage bores and cams. Lube outer face of the cams and support plate. Install original trust waster on front cam with new wave clip. Cams should spin smoothly in plate with no tight spots during rotation.

1. Install original or new inner chain tensioner. Use blue tread locker and torque the original bolts to 10 ft.lbs or 120 in. lbs.

4. Using specially designed tools, install new Torrington inner cam bearings...

2. Using specially designed tools, remove both inner cam bearings.

5. ...making sure the round side of the bearing faces in and the flat side with lettering faces out.

3. Clean and inspect bearing bores.

6. Lube and insert oil pump return O-ring in to the case. Be sure the O-ring is flat and square in the passage. Extra lube is a good thing here as it will ease the installation of the pump body later.

1. Next, insert oil pump body over pinion shaft. Align return spigot to engine case. Gently press spigot into case making sure not to twist or roll the O-ring.

4. Lube and insert inner return oil pump gear (the longer gear again) over pinion shaft and bottom out in pump body.

2. Lube up the pump body with clean oil or assembly lube.

5. Lube the outer portions of the return gears and slide in steel separator plate

3. Lube and insert inner return oil pump gear (the longer of the gears) over pinion shaft and bottom out in pump body.

6. Now slide in wave washer.

1. *And the second separator plate. Apply lube to outside of separator plate.*

4. *Install new feed and return O-rings.*

2. *Lube and install small inner oil feed gear.*

5. *A little pre-lube is a good idea, before the assembled support plate is slipped into place.*

3. *Lube and install outer oil feed gear, rotating it to line with inner gear*

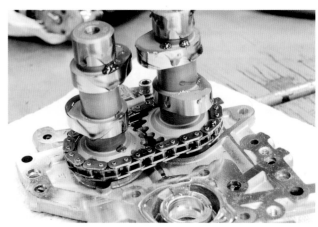

6. *Lube camshaft lobes and bearing surfaces.*

1. Lube inner cam chain and pinion shaft hole.

2. Gently slide support plate into camchest. DO NOT FORCE.

3. Install support plate bolts (not the 4 oil pump bolts) using blue Loctite. All 6 are the same length on the H-D plates. Torque to 10 ft.lbs. using a cross pattern. Verify that cams spin freely. The next step is easier with an extra set of hands.

1. While someone turns the engine forward, hand tighten the 4 oil pump bolts using a cross pattern - this will help center the oil pump components. Once hand tight, (and using the X pattern again) torque bolts to 10 ft.lbs. Spin engine over after to feel for any binding.

2. Lube and install original thrust washer on rear cam. These washers come in various thicknesses, note caption #1 on the next page.

3. Slide cam and pinion sprockets on the shafts. Note the alignment of the timing marks.

1. Using a straight edge and feeler gauge check the offset between the two sprockets. There should be no more than .010 in of difference. If greater install under or oversized thrust washer to correct.

4. Time now to reinstall the tensioner.

2. Now install sprockets with cleaned original or new chain. Rotating engine and cams to align dots on sprockets. Verify alignment using a straight edge through center of camshaft and pinion shaft.

5. Lube outer chain and sprockets.

3. Install cleaned or new bolts and washers in cam and pinion shafts, (use red Loctite and clean the female threads too). While holding rear brake, torque cam bolt to 35 ft. lbs and pinion bolt to 25 ft.lbs.

6. Install cam cover with new gasket. In a cross pattern, torque cover hardware with blue Loctite on threads to 10 ft. lbs or 120 in. lbs.

1. This picture of the lifters torn apart is to show that I check the lifters even new. It sucks, putting an engine together and have a stuck hydraulic lifter and need to pull it out.

4. After coating the lifter bodies with oil...

2. More pre-lubing, the lifter bores here...

5. ... all 4 lifters can be slipped into place.

3. ... then the lifter rollers.

6. With a new gasket in place, the 4 Allen bolts that hold the lifter block covers are tightened to 90 to 120 in. lbs.

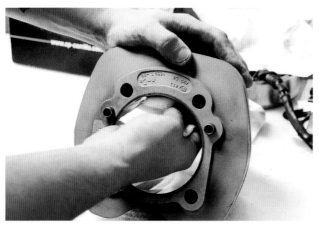

1. At this point, the cylinders have been honed to the tight dimension, and washed out thoroughly with soap and water. Before assembly, each cylinder gets wiped down with an oil-soaked rag.

4. If the ring gap is too tight, this handy little grinder will take material off each end of the ring.

2. The ring gap needs to be checked for both the upper rings - the piston is used to push the cylinder straight down into the cylinder...

3. ... so that the ring gap can be checked as shown. For a street engine, the recommended ring gap is .004 to .0045 inches per inch of piston diameter.

5. With a coating of oil on the bushing in the upper end of the connecting rod, and the piston pin, light pressure from your thumb should be enough to slide the pin into place. Remember, the pistons have to face the right way.

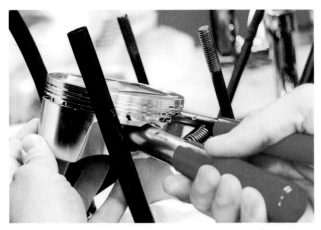

1. Jon uses a piston pin retaining ring installation tool here, though it can also be done without the tool. Be sure the retaining rings (circlips) snap fully into the intended recess.

4. Before sliding the cylinders in place, the pistons and rings need to be pre-lubed. Remember to space the ring gaps per the instructions that came with the rings.

2. Piston pins and retaining rings are in place, time for piston ring installation...

5. Next, compress the rings, leaving a little of the piston top sticking out...

3. ... which starts at the bottom of the piston. Be sure to follow the directions that come with the rings, they're not all the same.

6. ... after applying a coating of oil in the cylinder, carefully set it down on the top of the piston.

1. Don't force the cylinder, just ease it down over the piston and rings with pressure, and a few light blows, from your hand.

4. Note the brass reinforcing ring.

2. One cylinder in place, lock it there with two nuts placed on the studs as shown.

5. Assuming (always dangerous) that the heads have been serviced and all the gasket surfaces are clean...

3. At this point, it's time to check the distance from the cylinder gasket surface, to the top of the piston.

6. ... it's time to set the heads in place. Be sure to note any instructions that came with the head gaskets you use.

1. Put a light coat of oil under the head of the fastener, and on the internal threads, to ensure the torque readings are correct.

4. In this picture I'm drilling the drain holes in the stock rocker arm perches to 1/16 in. to allow better oil drain back from the breather valve to decrease oil misting.

2. We use a different method here for torquing head gaskets. We mostly use Cometic MLS (multi layer steel) gaskets, and torque them as follows: We start at 9 ft, lbs., then 22 ft. lbs., 35 ft. lbs., and 42 ft lbs.

5. Time to set the rocker box gaskets in place.

3. After the heads are fully torqued, we let them sit for approximately 30 to 45 minutes and retorque. This allows for gaskets settling and threads stretching.

6. The area around the valve spring has been opened up to accommodate the larger diameter valve springs as well as taller valve stem protrusion.

1. Using the oil can as an oil gun, inject oil into each rocker arm until it flows out the hole on the other end of the rocker arm.

2. At this point the rocker support is installed, while the pushrods have not. The 4 fasteners that secure the support assembly are tightened to 18 to 22 ft. lbs, the 6 perimeter fasteners to 120 to 168 in. lbs.

3. Apply assembly lube or grease to both ends of the pushrod tubes.

1. With new O-rings installed, insert pushrods into engine. The shorter of the two pushrods are the intake pushrods. Do not extend pushrods at this time.

2. While holding down the pushrods rotate the engine over slowly. The exhaust should open and close first, then the intake. Once intake closes continue to rotate engine slowly until piston is at TDC. Verify that both lifters are at their lowest, you should be at TDC on the compression stroke and can begin adjustment.

3. Extend pushrods by hand until they just touch the rocker arm and lifter's hydraulic center. Now extend pushrod .100 in. for standard lifters. The amount of turns will vary with different pushrods. Then lock the adjustment with the locking nut. Allow engine to set until - you are able to spin the push-rods easily by hand. If you can't, allow to sit longer. It can take time for extra oil in lifters to bleed out. NEVER rotate the engine if you can't spin pushrods by hand, - this can cause valve damage. And always adjust one cylinder at a time.

1. Before installing throttle body, using Vaseline, lube up both intake seals.

4. Progressively tighten the intake bolts until the seal flange is tight to the heads.

2. Insert throttle body between heads being careful that the seals stay in place. Insert all four bolts by hand.

5. Be sure to install all fasteners.

3. Align the throttle body so it is square to the engine.

6. Note the new exhaust gasket. The type of gasket (flat or tapered) depends on the shape of the pipe end. Note the pipe end shown on the next page.

1. Yes, the exhaust gasket must match the shape of the pipe's flange.

4. After all the pieces are hung, tighten everything up gradually...

2. Time to start hanging the exhaust...

5. ... working from the front to the back.

3. ...piece by piece, including the bracket shown here.

6. The aircleaner is next, remember the Loctite.

1. The breather hoses are attached to the heads with banjo bolts as shown.

3. ... positioning the hoses as you do.

2. Tighten each fastener...

4. All that's left is to finish installing the air cleaner cover.

5. Double check to be sure there's oil in the engine, and then it's time to fire it up.

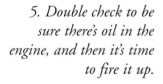

Chapter Four

Bottom End Assembly

Start from Scratch

The bottom end of your V-Twin, that is, the flywheel assembly and the engine cases themselves, are a lot like the foundation of your house. When you build a house, if the foundation ain't right, nothing else will be right either.

In this case we are following along as Jon from R&R Cycles assembles the bottom end for one of their 124 inch motors. Though the cases are from Harley-Davidson, most of the other components are R&R originals.

The cases that R&R uses for their 124 inch motors come from Harley-Davidson.

The cases used here are the cast cases meant for 110 inch motors, each set of cases has its own MSO (Manufacturer's Statement of Origin). They come with the roller bearings for the crank, and the inner cam bearings already installed (more on these later).

Because this is a high performance big-inch motor. the assembly will include installation of Timken crank bearings on the sprocket side. As Jon explains, "The Timken bearings really help to stabilize the crankshaft."

As is the case with most of the procedures in this book, even though the work seen here is done on a R&R engine using many of their own components, the procedures are essentially the same for a stock Harley-Davidson Twin Cam.

Installing the Timken bearings requires the use of a special insert in the left side case. At R&R they like to use longer installation screws for the insert, which requires a machining operation. Jon explains that, "it's just something we do. For everyone else, the standard machine screws can be used and then the whole operation can be done with only a drill press and no need for the CNC."

Because the engine being assembled will displace 124 cubic inches (4.125 inch bore and 4.625 stroke) not 110 (with a 4 inch bore) there are a few more necessary machining operations - and these can't be done with a drill press. The longer-than-stock connecting rods require more clearance inside the cases. Likewise, the oversize cylinders come with oversize spigots, meaning the recesses in the cases for the H-D 110 inch cylinders aren't nearly big enough. Luckily, at R&R they have a number of CNC machines, and they have Tim.

Because they build so many 124 engines, Tim has the CNC programmed for both machining operations. The third operation is of a more manual nature, and requires nothing more high tech than a lathe and competent operator. The big-bore cylinders and the necessary extra material taken out to accommodate

1. Jon starts with a set of virgin 110 cases from Harley-Davidson.

2. The first job is to split the cases, and take out the oil squirters...

3. ... the cases come with roller bearings installed for the crank.

1. Jon sets the case on this support.

2. Before the stock roller bearing

3. ... is pressed...

those cylinders mean that the center case bolt, the one that sits right in the V, needs to be necked down as shown in the nearby photo.

The use of the Timken bearings in the left side case requires a set up procedure to ensure the crank is installed without too much end play or preload. To set up the crank correctly requires another JIMS tool, spacers of various thicknesses, and patience on the part of the technician.

The right side case requires no special bearing insert, though Jon does knock out both the roller bearings for the crank, and the inner cam bearings. After a thorough cleaning of the case, and before final assembly, the roller bearing is replaced with Harley's Screamin' Eagle version. The standard cam bearings are replaced with Torrington bearings, which have roughly twice the number or rollers as do the stock bearings.

Before final assembly, the mating surface of each case half gets a thin coating of Three-Bond. Then it's assembly time, as best shown by the photo sequence that follows.

4. ... out of the left-side case.

1. Both of the bearings will be replaced. for the left side case the roller bearing will be replaced with a set of Timken bearings. Not shown, after complete disassembly comes a thorough washing.

4. The two-part tool, and insert...

2. Installation of the Timken set requires installation of the special inset, which in turn requires the use of the JIMS tool shown here.

3. The inset itself comes from JIMS as well...

5. ... fit together precisely as shown in this mock-up shot.

3. *Before installing the insert, Jon puts green Loctite on the smaller-diameter lip only...*

1. *One piece of the special tool mounts to the outside of the left side case, and is held in place by the fasteners that go into the existing holes in the case (which are there to mount the stator).*

2. *Here you can see that half of the tool from the other side.*

5. *... and oil on the larger-diameter part of the insert.*

1. The small hole in the insert lines up with the pin on the tool - note the arrow. And the larger pin on this half of the tool interfaces with the corresponding hole in the other half of the tool.

3. Jon drives the insert into place until he can feel that it's fully seated...

2. The press is used again to install the JIMS insert.

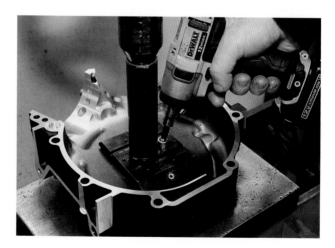

4. ... then locks it in place with an Allen bolt.

1. Once the insert and tool are fully seated and locked in place...

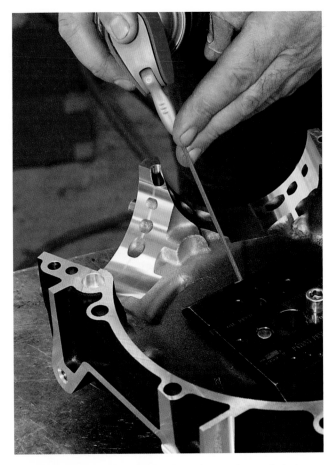

3. Jon starts with a little WD-40 used as a lubricant for the drilling...

2. It's time to drill the oil holes with the two drill bits shown - note the two guide holes in the tool.

4. ... followed by the drilling itself. Jon drills until the drill is all the way through.

1. Before pulling off the inner half of the tool, Jon vacuums up the shavings left from the drilling.

2. Next the tool itself is pulled out...

3. ... leaving the outer half of the tool still in place.

4. First the small machine screws are removed.

5. Then light pressure from the press is used to push the outer half of the tool out of place.

6. As mentioned in the text, R&R adds a step to the installation of the insert - they use a longer screw with a slightly different head shape. So ...

1. ... instead of just drilling and taping holes with a drill press at this point, the case is moved to a CNC ...

2. At this point Jon switches sides, and begins by knocking the stock cam bearings out of the right side case...

2. ... which is programed to drill and tap the holes. And change the shape of the countersink-taper slightly to accommodate the machine screws used by R&R.

4. ... using the appropriate driver and a medium sized hammer.

1. Net to come out will be the stock big roller bearing. The replacement, Screamin' Eagle bearing with the dark housing, will be installed instead.

2. Again, the press and necessary drivers, are used to push the crank roller bearing out of the case.

3. Clean, clean, clean - it's a three-step process: First the solvent tank, then the ultra-sonic cleaner, followed by a rinse in hot water...

4. ... and to quote Jon, "cleanliness is very important throughout this process."

1. Back to the left-side case, Jon puts a dab of Loctite on the machine screws before locking the insert in place.

3. Look closely, you can see the bearing race Jon just installed, as he removes the installation tool.

2. The Timken bearing set, with the bearing races and a spacer, come with the insert.

4. The left side case complete with insert, and the races for the outer and inner Timken bearings, installed.

1. Like the older H-D wheel bearings, the end play and pre-load of the Timken bearings is determined ...

2. ... by the thickness of a shim. The shim sent with the bearings isn't always the right one, so Jon does a mock up using a test sprocket shaft as shown. This shaft has been turned down, so the outer bearing will slide into place and doesn't need to be pressed onto the shaft.

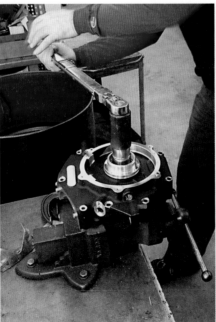

3. After the test shaft (with bearing and spacer in place) is inserted from the other side, Jon puts the outer bearing in place...

4. ... followed by a spacer, before torquing the nut down to factory specs.

5. Time now to check the feel of the bearing by rotating, and pushing and pulling, on the case.

1. The ideal is: "no end play, and very minimal pre-load." Here there's too much end play, so John measures the spacer he used and picks a thinner one. Then checks he fitment again, and maybe again.

2. Jon disassembles the mocked up case, and installs the new spacer...

3. ... and torques the nut to spec. Jon's done this numerous times, and the new spacer gives him the fitment described above.

4. Now the bearings and the correct spacer can be transferred to the real flywheel assembly. But first Jon installs this double male adapter (part of the special JIMS bearing install tool) to the end of the crank.

5. Here's the tool in action, installing the inner Timken bearing on the sprocket shaft.
Captions

1. Here's the sprocket shaft complete with the bearing and spacer installed.

3. ... followed by the outer Timken bearing...

2. Next, the left-side case is dropped in place...

4. ... which needs to be pressed on with the installation tool.

1. After giving the outer bearing a squirt of oil...

3. And now the tool is used...

2. ... it's time to slide the seal, and the adapter for the special tool over the shaft.

4. ... to push the sprocket seal into place as shown.

1. To avoid clearance issues between the pistons and the oil-squirters,

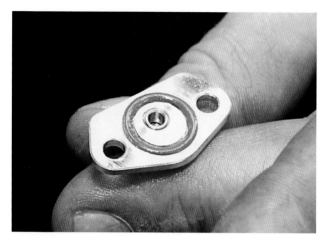

. ... R&R uses S&S squirters held in place with the machine screws from H-D. Don't forget the O-rings.

3. Before the right-side case can be mated to the right-side case, Jon installs a new Screamin' Eagle...

4. ... roller bearing for the crank.

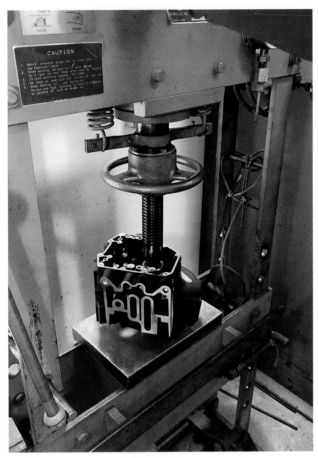

1. The right-side bearing needs to be pressed into place...

3. Actually the bearing is held in by two fasteners...

2. ... as shown here. Note the vacant tapped holes.

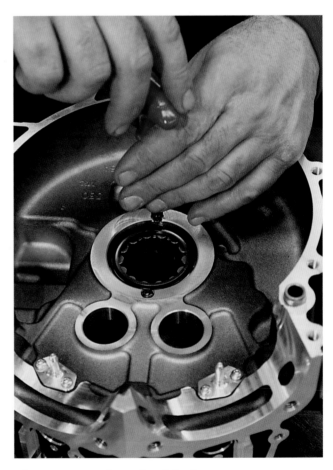

4. ... one on either side of the bearing.

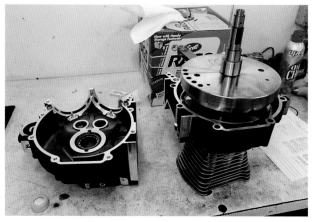

1. *Time to take stock and ensure the gasket surfaces are clean and free of nicks...*

4. *Now the case halves can be mated up.*

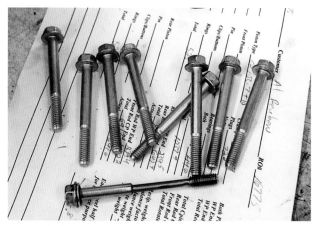

2. *And that all the engine-case bolts are present and accounted for. Note the necked down center bolt.*

5. *And after a few taps from a rubber mallet to ensure the cases are fully mated, Jon carefully snugs up the case bolts with a low-power electric impact wrench.*

3. *A thin coat of Three-Bond (the same product as Yama-Bond) is spread on both case halves.*

6. *Final tightening is done with a torque wrench set to 20 ft. lbs. - except for the center bolt which is tightened to only 10 ft. lbs.*

1. The cylinder studs are from H-D, and come with locking compound already applied to the threads. Jon prefers a different brand of locking material, so he wire-brushes the factory compound off.

2. ... before applying his own brand of compound to the treads...

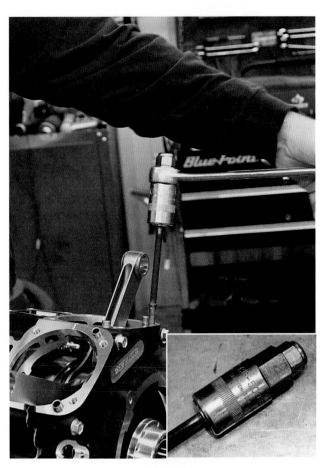

3. ... and screwing them in with a Snap-On stud installation tool.

4. One finished engine case ready for cylinder, heads, cams and all the rest.

4A H-D Bottom End Assembly

Rebuilding the bottom end of this Harley-davidson Twin Cam start with the removal of the old bearings.

Though it might seem redundant, we've decided to give readers two bottom end assembly sequences. The more detailed of the two makes up most of chapter Four. As that sequence is based on mostly R&R components and includes the installation of Timken bearings on the crank's left side, we give you sequence number two.

Unlike the sequence number one, this one is pure Harley-Davidson, using a stock Harley flywheel assembly supported by nothing more complex that the INA roller bearings on either side.

As you can see, it's pretty simple. First, you have to get rid of the original crank bearings which are pressed into the case. In order to do this correctly you need the tool from JIMS, shown in a nearby photo, and a press.

Removing the old bearings, without removing a significant amount of aluminum from the case at the same time, calls for a trick shared with us by Jon. "When those bearings have been in the cases for a lot or miles," explains Jon, "they're hard to get out without damaging the case. What I do is soak the seam between the outer race and the case, for a number of days if possible. The penetrating oil I like is Aerokroil."

"When I take the time to do this (to both the right and left cases) the old bearings come out without dragging any aluminum along the way, leaving a nice clean bore behind."

We are left with two bare cases which have been thoroughly cleaned and inspected.

4A H-D Bottom End Assembly

The bearings used for this installation are the Screaming Eagle INA Roller bearings with the black outer race - in fact it seems that Harley has discontinued the use or sale of the standard, non-SE bearings altogether. At any rate, there is no way to check the clearance.

About all you can do is check the diameter of the race that's pressed onto the crank - the INA bearings don't come with an inner race, the roller rely on the race that's on the crank.

Once the bearings are installed in the cases and the retaining machine screws are installed in the right side case, it's really a pretty simple installation.

2. The right-side crank bearing uses machine screws on the outside to retain the bearing in its bore. The inner cam bearings will be installed a little farther along in the assembly sequence.

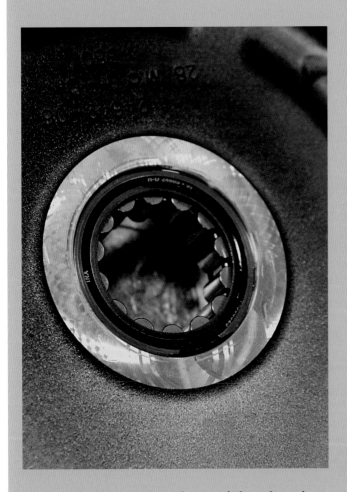

1. Once the bare cases are clean and then cleaned again, it's time to install new Screamin' Eagle roller bearings with the black outer shell.

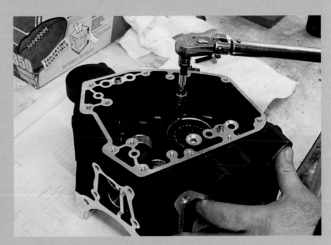

3. The machine screws are coated with a dab of red Loctite and then rightened to 10 to 12 ft. lbs.

4A H-D Bottom End Assembly

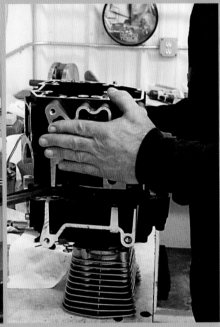

1. There is no real way to check the clearance between the crank and the bearing. If the inner race on the crank meets the spec you're ready to rock n' roll.

2. After pre-lubing the bearings, the left-side case is set over the crank assembly.

4. And the right-side is set in place.

3. Then the case is flipped over, Three-Bond is applied to both the sealing surfaces...

5. All that's left is to install the case bolts, and torque them to factory specs - and the bottom end is assembled.

Chapter Five

Flywheel Assembly & Balance

There are no Shortcuts

Shown here is the assembly of a complete R&R flywheel assembly. The assembly sequence shows the attention to detail exhibited by the R&R crew as they take two mainshafts, one crankpin, two flywheels, two connecting rods and various other components and assemble the whole thing into an incredibly strong, true and well balanced assembly.

Most of the flywheel assemblies in most of our V-Twin motorcycles are pressed together assemblies. Though the mainshafts may be integral to the flywheels or keyed to the flywheels (depending

Truing a V-Twin flywheel assembly requires a certain skill set, along with a lot of patience.

76

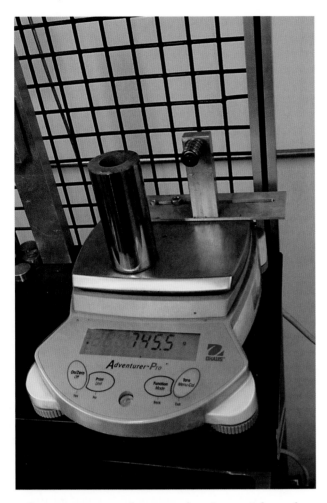

Before putting everything together, Jon weighs each individual part that makes up the crankshaft assembly.

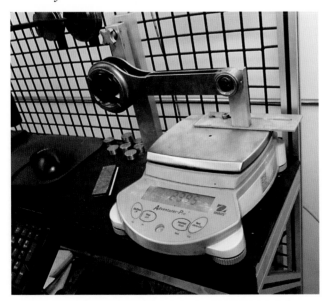

Connecting rods are weighed one end at a time.

on the manufacturer) what holds each flywheel to the crankpin is friction, there are no splines or keyways. Which means that under severe loads it is possible for one or both flywheels to shift slightly.

When motorheads talk about "welding the crank" what they mean is welding each flywheel to the pin, so that the 'wheels are much less likely to shift their position on the pin and relative to each other (note the photos at the end of the chapter).

Though the flywheel assembly sequence seen here is made up of R&R's own components, the basics of the assembly, and even the welding, holds true for nearly any Twin Cam flywheel - including the stock flywheel assemblies from Milwaukee.

As always, quality assembly starts with sub-components made from the best materials, machined to a very precise fit, and assembled with care in a very clean environment. Follow along as the crew at R&R Cycles show how they assemble a super durable flywheel assembly.

The Basic Assemble, True and Balance Sequence:

1. Weigh all the individual parts, note each weight.
2. Static Balance the two flywheel halves, individually - with the bob weight in place.
3. Take off material as needed, until the ideal static balance is achieved for each 'wheel.
4. Size both ends of the connecting rods.
5. Assemble the components, with shafts and keys, into a complete flywheel assembly using the special R&R fixtures.
6. True the assembly.
7. Press the plugs into the crankpin.
8. True the assembly again.
9. Weld the crank.
10. True the assembly again.
11. Do the dynamic balance of the complete crank assembly.

1. After weighing each end, Jon notes the weight of the entire rod.

2. The weight of each component is noted on the worksheet.

3. Each flywheel half is weighed individually, note the bob weight...

4. Flywheel halves are designed to be a bit heavy on the side opposite the pin recess. So in nearly all situations, material needs to be removed form the counter weight. The material is forges steel so this takes time.

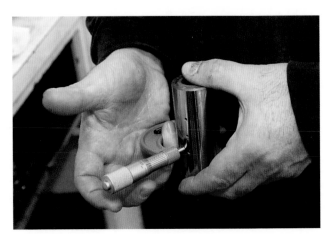

5. Before sizing the rods can begin, Jon needs to know the exact size of the pin.

1. As noted on this small worksheet, Jon likes to see the front rod with .0013 inches of clearance and the rear with .0015.

3. Jon goes through a series of sequences: measure, hone...

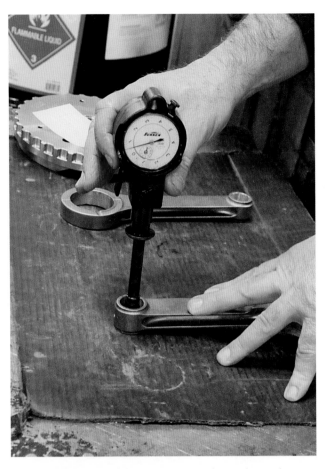

4. ... measure and hone again. Before taking the final reading Jon let's the rod cool off so the dimension is accurate and not affected by heat from honing. The final size is dependent upon engine size and application: street, race or both.

2. The measuring tool is made by the same company that manufactures the resizing/honing machine - Sunnen.

1. The fit should be snug enough that you can just push the pin through with light pressure.

3. Using the Sunnen hone and measuring function...

2. As with the rod's small-end, sizing is a matter of measure, hone and measure again.

4. ... Jon's rod fitment is accurate down to the ten-thousandths of an inch.

5. Missing the crank pin, but otherwise the components needed to assemble one complete R&R crankshaft assembly.

1. Because no one makes and sells the equipment needed to press together a V-Twin crankshaft...

2. ... R&R had to build their own. These two specialized presses are over-built to ensure everything stays true during the actually assembly.

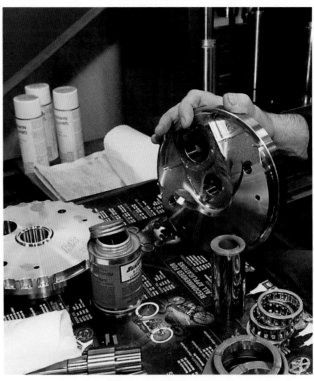

3. Jon starts by collecting all the parts he's going to need.

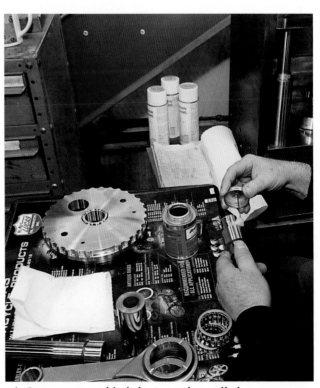

4. Sunnen assembly lube is used on all the components prior to assembly.

Q&A Jon Bird

According to Jon, doing quality work is simple: "You just gotta love what you do."

John: give us some background on you, how you became the guy who assembles most of the complete engines at R&R Cycles.

I started in road construction after high school, I got laid off every winter. When I was about 22, or 23, I decided I wanted something more, something that could become a career,

I bought my first Harley Davidson about that time. As soon as I started riding that thing a light bulb went on, I just wanted to learn how it worked. I was reading one of the bike magazines one day and saw this ad for AMI, American Motorcycle Institute. So I went and did that one winter when I was laid off. When I graduated I landed a job with Meredith Harley-Davidson, that was in 1986 and I've been doing it ever since.

You had your own shop for some time?

Yes, I had my own shop, that was always my goal. I worked for places like Meredith Harley-Davidson and Zipper's before that. Basically, I used those jobs as stepping stones. I needed education. The Harley shop was handy when I started because they didn't have an engine guy, and that was kind of where I wanted to be. I wanted to do stuff that made the bike go down the road. I wasn't interested in changing oil. It was the nuts and bolts that interested me, the engine and the transmission. I wanted to make it roar, go faster. Luckily the people at Meredith had faith in me.

I worked for myself for 15 years. I did mostly engine and transmission and driveline type of work. I did lots of machine shop stuff, boring and honing cylinders, valve jobs, a lot of what you see me doing now.

You build and assemble everything from street engines to full competition engines headed for Bonneville or the drag strip. What are some of the differences in the assembly procedures you follow for one, versus the other?

I think specialty engines, like something that you build for Bonneville where you're using components you've never laid hands on before, you have to do lots of checking. You have to make mock ups, check the pistons, that they don't run into each other at bottom dead center. Check valve-to-piston clearance, things like that. On those competition engines you really have to check everything that moves in the engine before final assembly.

And you have to adjust the clearances to work in the environment that the engine will live in. Two motors, one that goes to Bonneville and one that runs on the street, are going to survive with different running clearances,

Q&A Jon Bird

The engines that come out of R&R, whether an essentially Stock Harley 103 or a more radical 131 from R&R, have a very good reputation for longevity and durability, even in the hands of someone who rides hard. To what to you attribute the durability of those engines?

In the facility where I work, we have the capacity to develop parts of our own if we don't like what's commercially available. Crankshafts for instance. No one at R&R wanted to get into the crank business. But because we couldn't buy anything we were happy with, we were forced to make our own. The fact that we have this facility, means we can design and manufacture parts from the ground up.

And we have a good crew. They bring in people who have experience, who contribute to the final product. It's not a dictatorship, we all have input to the design and outcome of the final product. You also have to consider the experience and attention to detail shown by the guys who do assembly. And of course we do a lot of testing.

Good people and good equipment can create new, quality parts, out of nothing. As I mentioned, our crankshafts are a good example. We developed everything including the tooling and fixtures.

Here's the flip side of the same question: you see a lot of damaged engines come into the shop, what are some of the failures you see most commonly - and how could those failures have been prevented?

The sad part of this business is the fact that a five dollar mistake can create a five thousand dollar event. Some of those shops that had a problem are at an unfair disadvantage. They buy kits from someone else, and don't have all attention to detail, or know how much attention to detail that is needed, to put that kit together so that it will survive.

It goes back to having the experience with a set of parts, to understanding the correct clearances, and the things you need to check. You also need the facilities to machine the things you need to machine. And you need the experience to know what will work and what won't.

There's a great deal of controversy about bottom ends, on stock and modified Harleys. When you plan a

hop up on one of these, at what point do you need to consider a welded crank, and/or a set of Timken bearings on the sprocket side?

A lot of people do it when they're in the bottom end anyway. If you're going to go into the bottom end because of wear or because of the engine modifications being done, it makes sense to do it while you're in there. When we do modifications, like a 124 kit, at that point we wouldn't consider leaving out the Timkens and the welding and the balance.

With more modest upgrades, like a 96 inch engine getting a big-bore 103 or 107 kit, I don't think that we tear the crank out unless there's another issue. Things like how old is the bike and the crank? What's the runout now? But if we do decide to do one thing, like weld the crank, then it makes sense to do the other, the Timken bearings, at the same time.

On the top end, what are the things to watch out for during assembly? You talk a lot about the clearances?

The piston to cylinder wall clearance is most important of all the clearances. Because there again you have a very narrow window, too tight it will stick. Too loose, and it will rattle. The final clearance to come up w the numbers I use, I need skill, good measuring tools and good machines to do the machining.

Those clearances are temperature sensitive. I need a good understanding of what will happen when I walk away from the machine. But I do walk away and let the cylinders, or connecting rods, cool off - rod bearing clearance is the second most important clearance. So I don't measure them when they're hot, because the reading I get won't be accurate. It's so important to the longevity of the components that are essential to the longevity of the engine.

This is a little redundant, but what are the things that you've learned to do or be careful with, that other builders and mechanics sometimes miss?

You gotta love what you do. When you get to the point where you really care about what you do, then the things I talk about become second nature.

1. Pressing the pinion shaft...

2. ... into the right side flywheel half is the first item on the assemble list.

3. These locating holes are bored during the final machining operations and will be used to locate the flywheel during additional operations.

4. Next, Jon positions the left side flywheel...

5. And presses the sprocket shaft...

6. ... into place here.

1. Jon is marking where the oil hole is. He will also mark the oil hole location in the crank pin and then align the two marks when he presses the pin into place.

2. ... applying the Sunnen assembly lube

3. ... to both the flywheel and the crank pin...

4. ... next the pin is positioned....

1. ... and then pressed into the right-side flywheel half.

3. ... and then put the rods in place on the crank pin.

2. Time now to assemble the connecting rod bearings with the rods themselves...

4. Before proceeding further, the sub-assembly is pulled out of the press, and the pin is lubed...

1. ... before being placed in the horizontal press as show.

4. ... and positioned so the crank pin will line up perfectly...

2. A big C-clamp is used to hold the sub-assembly in place...

5. ... with the right side flywheel half.

3. ... and then the left side flywheel half is lowered into place....

6. Now, Jon can lift the crank assembly out of the horizonal press...

1. ... prior to beginning the truing operation.

3. ... all part of getting the two shafts true...

2. The tool shown is used to squeeze the flywheel halves together...

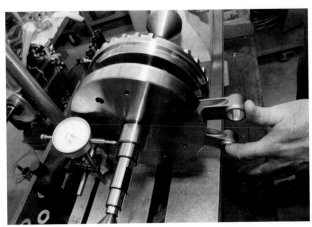

4. ... ideally with no more than .001 inches of runout.

1. Jon is holding one of the plugs used to fill the end of the crank pin.

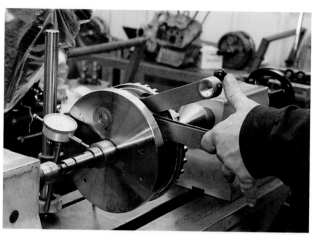

3. Time now to check that the crank assembly is still true, and adjust it if it isn't.

2. The next step is to press the plugs into the pin on either side.

4. You've heard people talk about "welding the crank," well this is what they mean...

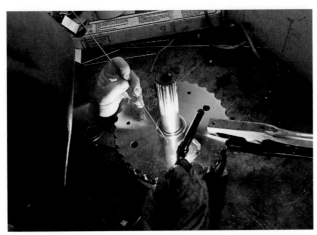

1. ... done by Chris the porting expert with the Heli-arc welder, "I use pure Argon, and set the welder at 175 amps," explains Chris. "I use a 2% thoriated tungsten, with a 1/16th inch ER 70S2 welding rod."

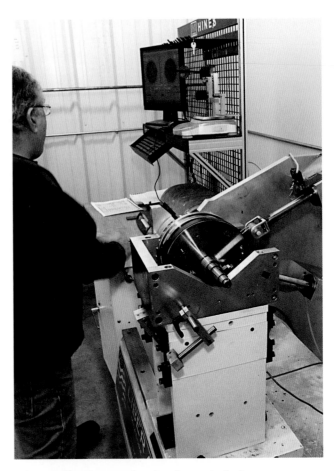

4. Finally it's time for the dynamic balance....

2. After knocking down the weld bead Jon mounts the assembly in the truing fixture.

3. Every time something is done to the crank it's likely to change the dimensions - so now it's time to true it just one more time.

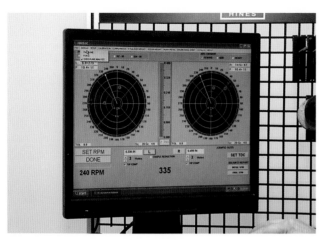

1. *The screen shows force and couple (influencing one side of the wheel or the other) will balance the force and couple under 1 gram total. There are many sensors on the balancer, which helps to make it truly accurate.*

3. *Then it's back on the balancer.*

2. *After the initial run, Senior uses the drill press to removed material from the right side flywheel.*

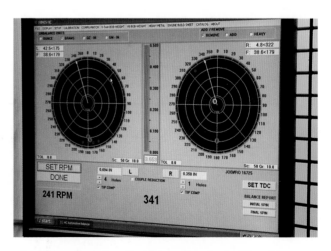

4. *The end goal, a final run that looks like this.*

Chapter Six

Top End Assembly

Cylinders, Pistons, Rings

Like most parts of quality engine assembly, there is more to the top end assembly than just honing the cylinders, sliding the rings into place on the pistons, and then sliding the cylinders down onto the pistons.

In this case, the cylinders for this 124 R&R engine come from S&S. "We get them ten-under," explains Jon, "so there's plenty of extra meat and we can be sure to get them straight and to the correct size."

The first cuts are done on the CNC machine, followed up by the really important part of this assembly - the honing.

Cylinders for this 124 come from an outside shop, though R&R does the final sizing and honing.

After washing away the debris left from boring the cylinder, Jon mounts both cylinders to the fixtures that are part of the honing machine. Check the nearby photo and you will see that to mount the cylinders in the fixture Jon uses torque plates. The whole idea here is to ensure the cylinders maintain the same shape during honing that they have when they are torqued in place on the engine's bottom end.

In spite of the torque plates, the cylinders do move a certain amount as the hone comes by. As Jon explains it: "People don't realize that with these cylinders you can't just run the hone up and down and up and down, the liner has more support at the top, there isn't as much support at the bottom so the cylinder will get out of the way of the stones so to speak. The lower part of the cylinder, the spigots, moves as the stones come past, in those cases you have to spend more time with the stones at the bottom of the cylinder."

Before turning on the honing machine, Jon sets the bore gauge to read zero when the proper size is achieved by honing. It's all based on the diameter of the pistons. The goal is a final clearance of .0025 inches at room temperature.

Near the very end of the honing operation the stones are changed from a true stone to a finishing stone, which might best be described as a brush. "The final cross-hatch pattern is established by both the stones and the finish stones or brushes," explains Jon.

"For the last one-thousandth of an inch," says Jon, "I check the cylinder size a number of times. And I set up the hone to spend more time on the upper part of the cylinder. When I'm all done, it's all the same size down to .0002 inches or so."

Most of the actual putting-together of the top end is best explained by the photos, but there are two more fitment issues that bear mentioning.

First is the ring gap. A special little grinding tool is used at R&R to remove material from both sides of the gap on the compression rings. As shown, Jon takes off material, then slides the ring down into the cylinder. Before getting out the feeler gauge to check the gap, Jon positions the ring in the cylinder with an inverted piston to

After the initial sizing on the CNC, the cylinders move to the hone. Note the torque plates, the idea is to ensure the cylinders have the same shape here that they do when the engine is fully assembled.

ensure it's square in the bore. The specification here is .004 to .0045 inches per inch of bore, "this is the gap we like to see on these 124 engines running on the street," explains Jon. "If it's a turbo bike going to Bonneville, that's different."

The other fitment issue worth mention is the distance between the top of the piston and the combustion chamber. Near the end of the photo sequence you can see the gauge that's used to check this dimension. The ideal for this particular engine combination is a difference of .035 to .040 inches. This dimension is also affected by the thickness of the head gasket. Note the related caption information on this chapter's last page.

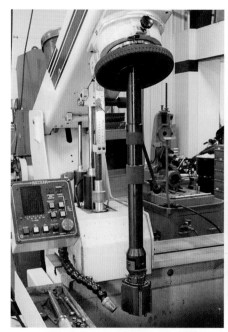

1. The hone has 4 diamond stones, mounted on a long arm. These are the cutting stones, not the finish stones mentioned in the text.

2. The goal is to get the cylinders straight, leave the necessary cross-hatch pattern, and...

3. ... get them to exactly the right size of course.

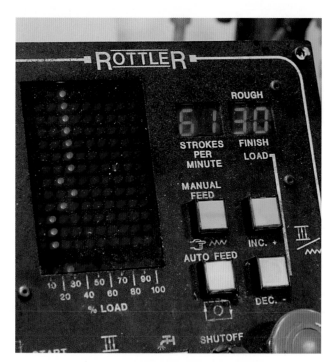

4. The hone is adjustable for rpm, as well as the up and down speed. The dot graph on the left shows how much load the stones encounter as they move up and down the cylinder from top to bottom. More load in one area means the cylinder is a little smaller at that point.

5. Jon is also able to adjust the machine so the hone spends more time in one part of the cylinder, per comments in the text.

1. The bore gauge is adjusted to show zero as the perfect dimension. Jon measures the bore from the top to the bottom.

2. R&R starts the cleaning with soap and water, then uses the ultrasonic cleaner to remove all the grit and debris left from boring and honing.

3. Here's the pistons, rings and circlips. Remember to read the instructions that come with the rings.

4. An inverted piston can be used to position the compression rings, one at a time, in the cylinder when checking the ring gap - see the next page.

1. Once the ring is square in the cylinder, a feeler gauge can be used to measure the ring end gap.

2. This nifty little grinder is used to take material off both ends of the rings to increase the gap.

3. Check and double check. The goal is a gap of .004 to .0045 inch per inch of cylinder diameter.

4. Before installing the pistons, Jon lubes the piston pin bushing and the pin itself...

5. ... he also double checks the fit of the pin itself. Light thumb pressure should be enough to push the pin through the bushing.

1. Now the real McCoy. First, install the pin in the piston.

4. Not all rings are the same, it's important to follow the instructions.

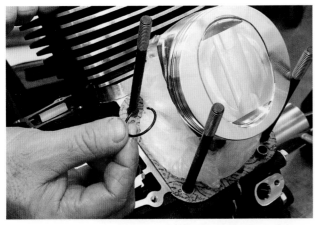

2. Next, the circlips. Note the base gaskets in place, and the plastic stuffed in the cavity below the piston - so the clip doesn't end up in the bottom of the cases.

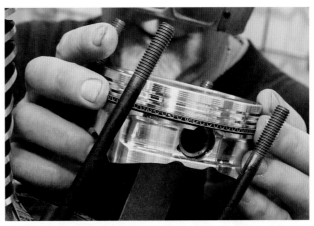

Because the recess for the pin cuts into the bottom ring land, this set of rings uses a 4 piece oil ring set.

3. ... Jon makes sure they are fully seated in the groove.

6. It's important to stagger the ring gaps so they don't line up. Jon positions the gap of the top 2 rings towards the intake side, to keep the ring-ends from getting too hot.

1. After oiling the rings and piston, it's time to...

3. After a little more oil, in the cylinder this time...

2. ... install the ring compressor, with a little bit of the piston protruding at the top.

4. ...he sets the cylinder over the piston ...

1. ... and uses a series of soft blows to push the cylinder past the rings and over the piston.

2. Once the cylinders are in place there's only one thing left to do for this part of the assembly.

3. And that one thing is to check the distance from the top of the piston to the cylinder's gasket surface. The ideal measurement is anywhere from .000 to .005 in. in the hole. This allows a gasket thickness of .030 to .036 to be used to achieve the proper squish.

4. Finished - except for just a few things like cylinder heads camshafts and all the rest.

Chapter Seven

Heads, Valves & Porting

It's All About Velocity

An entire book could be written on heads, ports, and that vague verb - "porting." And yes, entire books have already been dedicated to this topic that we are going to cover in one chapter divided up into roughly three separate sections: Building a head from scratch, the initial machining done with the CNC machine center, and the art and science of hand porting.

Though we are, again, dealing mostly with components designed by R&R and cast to their specifications, the basics of good port design and porting cross over to heads from other manufacturers like Harley-Davidson, and General Motors for that matter.

The R&R heads seen here are cast at an outside facility to R&R's own design and specifications.

Converting a raw casting into a working and well designed cylinder head requires a long series of steps. This close up shows a head half way through the valve job part of the process. Note the nicely shaped intake seat and the raw, uncut exhaust seat.

There's more to making a good head than you might think and some things about good port design are a bit counter intuitive, i.e. there is a such a thing as a port that's too big for a certain application. Because you need more than just volume, you also need a port that keeps the air-fuel mixture moving. In other words, you need velocity and volume.

At R&R the raw casting goes from the foundry to the powder coater. Once back to R&R with a fresh coat of texture black, the heads are set up on the CNC, one at a time. Externally, the fins are trimmed, the combustion chamber is machined to it's nearly-finished shape, and the gasket surface is milled to a nice smooth and perfectly flat surface. Internally, the shapes of the intake and exhaust port are cut out, and precise bores are cut for insertion of the valve seats and guides a little later.

Hand Work

From the CNC machines the heads are taken to R&R's in-house master of porting, Chris Cerasoolo. The CNC tools leave the combustion chamber and the ports with a fairly rough texture. Chris' initial goal is simply to eliminate the tooling marks. All this work is done before the seats and guides are installed, because as Chris says, "it's a lot easier to get around in there with the tools before the seats and guide are installed." From a pair of metal cutting bits, Chris moves to sand paper rolls until it's time to think about finishing the assembly.

Seats and Guides

After a thorough cleaning the heads go into the oven for a little baking at 350 degrees. The seats on the other hand go in the freezer. "I always put in the exhaust seat first," says Chris. "It's the hardest one to install because the tolerances are tighter." in the blink of an eye, first the exhaust and then the intake seats are installed in each head.

Guides are next, and while the seats need a fit with .0065 inches of interference, the guides and the heads are measured before installation to insure a fit with .0015 inches of interference. Both seats and guides are available in various oversizes.

Valve Job and Porting

If you've ever wondered why a good porting job costs as much as it does, you have only to follow along as a master goes through the multi-step process of first, the valve job, and then the actual porting - the sequence starts a little farther along.

1. R&R heads start life in the raw - casting is done at outside facility.

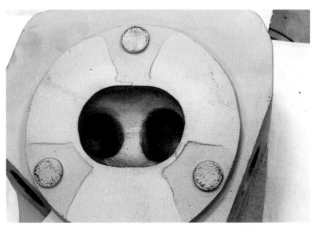

2. Yes, the ports are there, but there's a lot of material that needs to be removed on the CNC and by hand.

3. Once they're delivered to the shop, raw heads are placed on fixtures in the CNC machines.

1. The first set of operations...

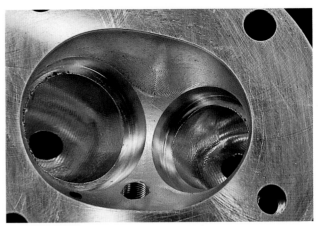

4. ... and bore holes for the guides, and an inset for the valve seats.

2. cleans up the outside of the heads - which are then sent out for powder coating.

3. Not only do the automated do the "CNC port-ing," they also drill and tap necessary holes...

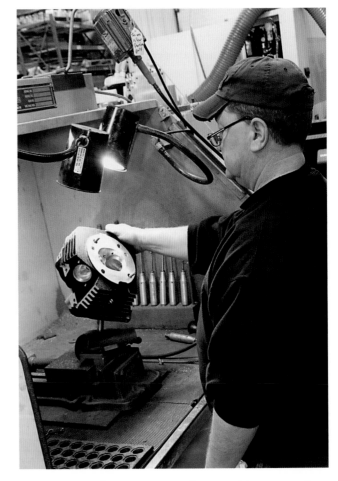

5. CNC machines are great, but machines are only so good. Once most of the material is removed from the ports, Chris up each head for the final porting work done by hand.

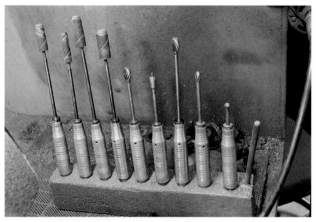

1. Chris' tools include everything from carbide bits meant to removed metal quickly, to sandpaper rolls in various grits.

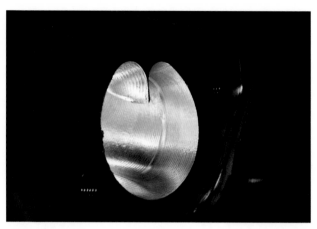

3. ... leaves a pretty rough surface.

2. The CNC tooling...

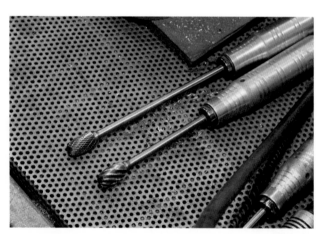

4. Chris starts with the coarse cutting tools...

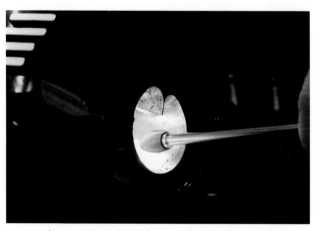

5. ... eliminating the ridges and taking out additional material in certain areas.

1. Most of Chris' porting work is done before the valve guides and seats are installed just because that way it's easy to get around in there with the tools."

3. Next comes work done with the sandpaper rolls...

2. Early in the hand-porting sequence - done with a carbide bit - the ridges seen early have been eliminated.

4. ... at this point most of the shaping is done. Next the seats and guides are installed and then the final finish work.

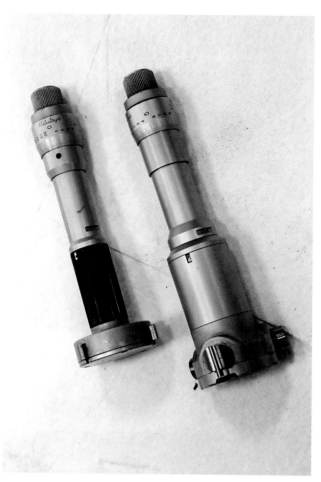

1. The first part of installing the valve seats is to measure the bore left by the CNC machine.

3. Here you can see the necessary tools - and the exhaust seats just out of the freezer wrapped up in the towel near the bottom of the photo.

4. Chris mounts the head on a fixture, note the Mitts, the heads just came out of the 350 degree oven.

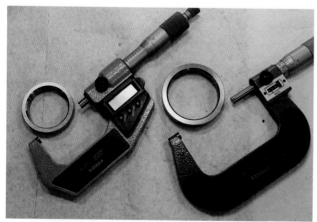

2. Valve seats come in various oversizes, Chris likes to have an interference fit of .0065 inches plus or minus .0005.

5. Before installation, the seat...

1. ... and the bore in the head are coated with the Sunnen lube.

2. Next, Chris holds the seat on the driver and slips driver and seat down into place...

3. Now it's time to drive it home.

4. Here we have two new seats, correctly installed, just before the start of the valve job.

Painless Valve Guide Removal

1. Using he cutting tool shown, in the valve grinding machine, Chris is able to neatly cut the valve guide off flush with the head.

2. Next, an air-chisel with a stepped tool is used to drive the guide out of the head.

3. Close examination will show that the gude too out very little alumium, on its way out of the head.

I noticed when I would hammer the valve guide out of a head, especially on Evo heads, but Twin Cams too, that they came out really hard. And by the time I beat hard on them for awhile with the tool and a hammer, the guide would actually swell up in size - and it would end up taking a lot of aluminum out of the head as I drove it out.

So then I had to use an oversize valve guide. I figured I had to come up with a better way of doing this.

So I started cutting the top of the guide off almost flush with the surface of the head, (check the nearby photos), and then I use an air chisel with a stepped tool (see the photos again), and the guides came right out. And if you look at them once they're out, you can see they don't take very much aluminum with them. It's a much better way of getting those old guides out of the head.

Copy: Chris Cerasoolo

Q&A: Chris Cerasoolo

Chris is one of those guys who's done it all, from building engines to racing both two and four-wheelers. But in the end, there is nothing Chris would rather do than port cylinder heads.

Chris, you've been porting heads all your life, how did you get started?

When I was 14 I acquired a 900 Kawasaki basket case, a Z-1. That brought me into the Kawasaki shop in Nashua, where they did a lot of drag racing. The first time I walked into the shop I was blown away. I thought, "I gotta do this."

They helped me with the assembly when I put that Z-1 engine together. The head mechanic showed me how to port the head, which meant I had to go out and buy the tools he recommended. That started the ball rolling.

Next I got a drag racing bike. This kid in town had a bike built just to beat me, but he crashed the bike right away and ended up selling it to my brother and me. After I got it back on the road the first thing I did was take it to the track. Eventually I blew the engine. So I went to buy a replacement cylinder head and it was 5000 dollars! - way out of my league. So I took a stock, head and copied everything they'd done to the broken head. And the bike ran great.

A couple of jobs later I went to work for Phil Miller, he was a very successful drag racer and ran a shop called Miller Machine. He was the first to break 200 mph in the quarter mile, that was about '65.

I started working there and suddenly I had this huge volume of heads to repair and port. Phil was such a big name that we had all this work. In fact, we did the heads for the Boston Strangler funny car.

I worked in a bunch of shops, and had a shop of my own for quite a while. I've built engines for all kinds of vehicles, but I always came back to cylinder heads - in the end it turns out I have a major passion for cylinder head work.

So, what are some of the major things you learned along the way? And are there some "rules" out there that turn out to be myths?

I leaned that the flow bench numbers aren't everything. It's a comparison. The flow bench is a good way to compare the flow I get before and after a porting job. But maximum flow means nothing. The flow at 1/2 cam lift means everything. At 45 degrees of crank rotation you're working on momentum, because of what's going on in the cylinder

Can you talk more about what's going on in the cylinder at 45 degrees of crank rotation and the importance of momentum?

At 45 degrees of crank rotation the piston is half way down the cylinder. After 45 degrees, another event is coming up, which causes reversion, It's the valve closing. Reversion is the enemy

Q&A: Chris Cerasoolo

of high velocity. You need velocity to create momentum - and overcome reversion.

I explain it this way. You have a bunch of people piled up in front of a door, you open that door and people will spill through as soon as the door opens. The shape of the port on the other side of the door has a big effect on how those people (or molecules of air) react and get through.

I can direct the air, I can tell the air molecules where to go. I can also create things that are in the way of the air, because that can create velocity. When it comes to creating any power, velocity is very important. That's definitely one of the most important things I've learned - a high velocity head is more important that high flow head.

Let's back up a little, go back to the basics, and talk about the sequence that you go through when you do a porting job?

Well, It goes like this:

1. Disassemble the head.
2. Degrease and glass bead, clean it.
3. Inspect the valves, the guides and the springs.
4. Decide what needs to be replaced.
5. Then, knowing what I need, it's time to have a discussion with the client. What do you ride, and how do you ride?
6. Then I can decide whether or not we need oversize valves and a bigger cam. If we do go for bigger cam, then I like to go with bigger valves at that point.

Usually oversize valves and a cam go along with a porting job, but I can also just open up those ports and create an increase in performance without the bigger valves and the wilder cam. I guess what I'm trying to say is, there's no one-size-fits-all kind of porting. You have to match the job to the other components and the kind of riding the owner does.

So, can you explain the difference in porting a Stage 2 kit and a Stage 5 kit?

With a Stage 2 job, we increase the size of the intake valve from 1.8 to 1.9 inches. I like to end up with a port that's in the mid 90s (the volume of the port in ccs). In the case of a Stage 5 head, we use a two-inch intake valve, and the intake port volume could be around 115cc volume. There's obviously a lot more metal removed with the Stage 5 head than a State 2 head. Again, the volume of the intake port must match the engine application.

How do you balance volume and velocity? You talk about the importance of velocity, but at the same time you're making the port bigger. How do you make the port bigger without making it too big and slowing down the velocity of the air moving through the port?

It's a balance between the rider, the engine, and the other engine components.

When you're porting, is there one part of the port that's more important than the rest, in terms of getting good flow and good performance?

A half an inch before and after the valve, those are the most critical areas. That is where you get the most bang for the buck.

We talked a little about the flow bench, do you need a bench to do good porting work - to check and measure the before and after airflow?

Yes, in order to port anything you need to be able to measure the before and after, you can absolutely ruin a port not knowing how to do it right.

Any tips for someone who's just getting started with porting?

If you want to understand how air moves, go to the river, to a corner and just watch what is happening. Take a leaf and throw it on top of the water and watch. Water and air, they flow pretty much the same. The way those air molecules move is similar to the water. The river comes down into a narrow area, as it goes through that narrow area the water will speed up. if it went off a cliff then you have volume.

1. Back to our cylinder head. Like the valve seats, there needs to be an interference fit between the head and the guide. Before installation it's important to clean the guides and the heads thoroughly.

2. I like .0015 inches of interference, "says Chris. "I don't want the guide to just fall into place."

4. ... before the head is moved to the press, where a special driver is set in place before the guide it driven home.

3. And like the seats, the guide and head are both coated with Sunnen lube...

5. With the guides in place Chris can do the valve job and final porting and polishing.

1. Reaming the valve guide is the first step before Chris can start with the true valve job can begin.

2. Chris uses the reamer, with the head in place on the valve grinding machine, and uses the machine's lubricant on the reamer as shown.

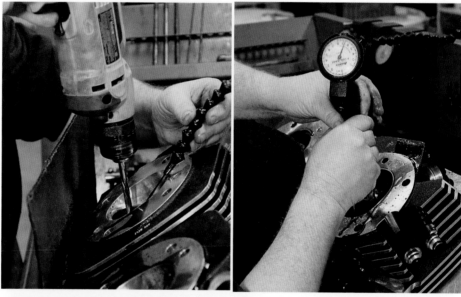

3. A variety of heads are available for cutting the seats of different sizes to different angles.

1. The tools-heads spin on these polished shafts - which come in different diameters to fit valve guides of nearly any size.

2. Both heads set up on the machine for the multi-step valve job.

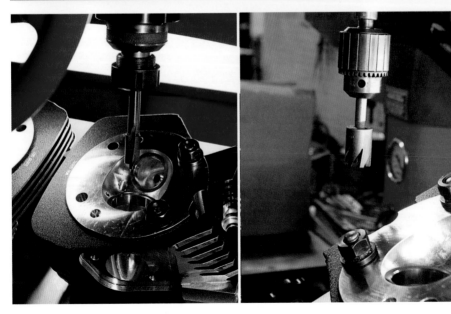

3. Once everything is in place and Chris knows the quill is on the same center-line as the valve guide, he uses cutters to trim the guide so it's sure to clear the head of the valve.

1. One virgin intake port.

4. Here's the seat after the third cutting operation.

2. The first cut is a vertical cut that simply enlarges the innermost diameter of the seat slightly - also a good way to ensure the seat and the guide are on the same centerline.

3. This is the seat after only two cutting operations, note how Chris is developing a radius seat for maximum air flow.

5. The nearly finished intake port, missing only hand porting, and blending where the seat meets the port and the combustion chamber.

1. Time now to finish off the combustion chamber.

3. Working with one of the fairly coarse pads...

2. For finishing the area where the port meets the chamber, and the chamber itself, Chris likes these mini abrasive pads, available in various grits from ???

4. ... Chris runs the pad over the entire combustion chamber.

5. It's not just a matter of polishing the chamber, a big part of Chris' work is to smooth out the lip where the port meets the chamber for good air flow.

114

1. *To back up a little: When it comes to porting 90% of it happens within 1/2 inch of the valve seat. That's where you have to concentrate your efforts.*

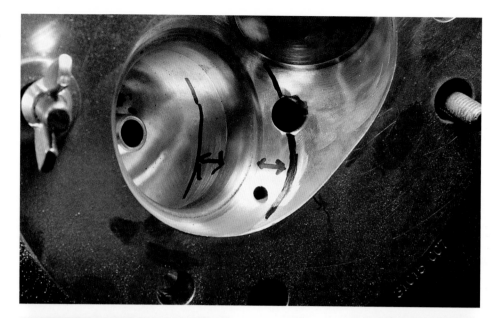

2. *The small diameter sandpaper roll is especially useful for eliminating the lip where the port meets the chamber.*

3. *Here you can see that Chris is moving to less aggressive pads...*

1. ... to eliminate any remaining machine marks, and swirls left by preceeding steps.

2. Back to the valve job. Chris uses the lathe to reduce the diameter ...

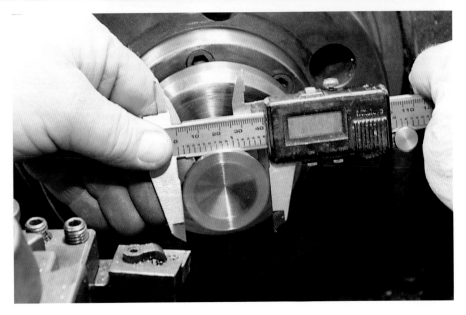

3. ... of the exhaust valve slightly.

1. Next, the valve is "faced," primarily so Chris knows the valve face is concentric with the valve stem.

2. Time now to clean the heads and components one last time, then drop the valves into their guide...

3. ... and install the valve springs and retainers.

4. After watching all the steps that are part of a good porting job, it's easy to see why a porting job, or complete set of heads cost as much as they do.

A Conversation with Senior

Working Outside the Box

What follows is a Q&A with Reggie Senior, the other half of the R&R partnership. When it comes time to design a new cylinder head, it's Reggie Senior who does the initial CAD drawings, which in turn become the blue print for the first prototype heads cut on the CNC. And it was Senior who did most of the initial design work on the V-Twin that powered Jody Perewitz to a long list of records. More engineer than biker, Reggie Senior is a man who's able to look past all the clichés and all the things that everybody "knows" in order to figure out what it really takes to make a V-twin haul ass, and stay alive doing it.

Senior, let's talk about designing a head from scratch - and the ports in particular.

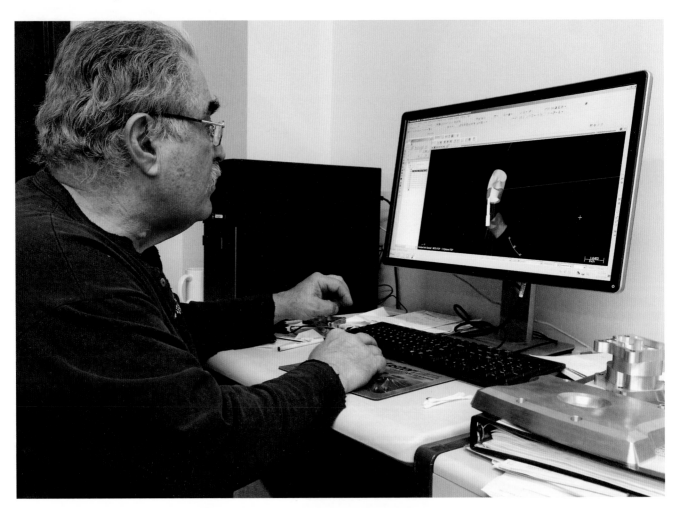

Senior is the one key member of the R&R team who spends as much time at the computer as he does in the shop.

You said once that when you're designing a head, you start with the ports?

Yes. I make sure the heads work intrinsically within themselves. For example, if we let in a quart of air, we want to let out a quart of air out - at the right time. We don't want to let the quart out too early and we don't want to not let all the air out.

If the air is let out at the right time then everything is good. That will be determined by port design, cam timing and valve size. Also, the port needs to be sized to both fit the valves and match the engine's application.

We design heads to work. We bring as much intake in as we can for that particular engine. Example, we do a calculation, if we think that at 6000 rpm, the engine needs 325 CFM of air, we will size the valve and port for the 325 CFM. That is how we start. We define the engine size - the minimum and maximum displacement - and the application, then we design the ports to fit that engine. We don't want them too small, but we also don't want it where we have too big a port for too small an engine, because at low RPM you can't keep the fuel atomized and then you're burning the charge instead of combusting (more on combusting vs. burning later).

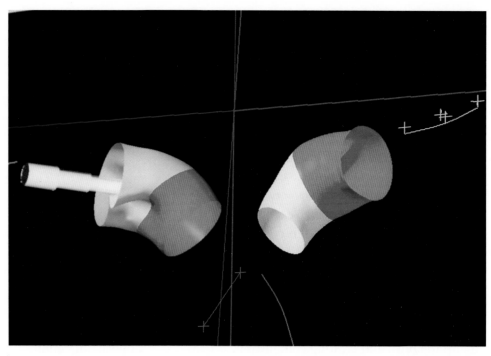

Picture of cad designed head ports with porting tool checking for any tool shank interference and cusps machined and oriented correctly.

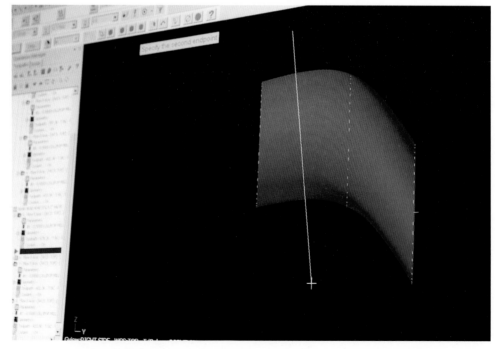

Here we are analyzing port volume and orientation.

You also said that when it comes to ports, velocity is more important than volume. That sometimes a smaller valve and port can be more useful than a bigger one?

First, let me say, fuel injection compensates for ports that are really too big to work at lower rpms, because the fuel injection atomizes the fuel (the injection nozzles break the gas into a fine mist of very small particles that atomize easily).

Now I will explain why velocity is so important. If the intake port and valve are too big for the engine the fuel will drop out of suspension at low RPM. The fuel will ball up like a fist, and when it gets to the cylinder it burns, it doesn't combust. Burning is slower. When you open your fist, it's easy for the oxygen to get between the fingers, all the fuel is ignited at the same time, speeding up the burn and creating combustion.

Let's look at the time from one piston cycle to another, you may only burn half the fuel. And you only get half the power. The fuel that doesn't get converted to energy becomes heat. You elevate the temperature of the head, and the oil gets overheated. The oil looses its lubricity and you get lubrication problems. Complete combustion keeps the engine cool. The engine runs cool at low RPM and the oil stays cooler.

Velocity is very important for the street rider because it will keep that engine cool and you end up with more torque at lower RPM. And you will extend the life of the engine because the oil is not super heated and therefore can lubricate the engine as it should.

Quoting you again, you said that in terms of a well designed port, you need one chokepoint in the port, and then a two to four degree wall going either way. Why do you need the choke point in the first place?

Let me start by inhaling a big breath. Even though I'm pulling air into my mouth and lungs, you can hear it from a foot away. What you hear is a series of pressure waves that were sent out in the opposite direction.

Where a choke point becomes very important is in terms of added cylinder fill. When the piston pulls downs fast, when the rod is moving through 90 degrees of crank rotation, that's where the piston is moving the fastest in the cylinder. As it moves through that 90 degree point, that's where it really sucks and it sends that expansion wave (that starts within the port) up the intake tract - where it reflects off the atmosphere and starts back toward the valve as a compression wave.

And if it's timed just right, that compression wave will come back toward the cylinder, just before the intake valve closes. As it moves towards the valve, it pushes a lot of additional charge into the cylinder. You get a super-charging effect.

Now, picture an hourglass lying on its side with the choke point in the middle. That choke point speeds up the air moving through the choke, but on the other side of the choke the air is

Testing flow characteristics of different valves on super flow 600 bench. All depression checking is done on Super Flow 1050 bench or a highly modified bench for depressions over 100.

moving slower and it's pressurized. If the choke point in a port is designed properly (remember, a real port has all kinds of turns and restrictions) the pressure will end up pushing the fuel air around the valve so you're flowing all of the valve not just part of the valve.

The choke point does a few things. Obviously it's not perfectly round like the hourglass, so the choke point needs to be the right shape. That's why we put shapes in the port. So that after it goes through the choke point, the air-fuel will move at the right speed to flow all the valve.

Shops sometimes size the intake valve bigger to get all the air that the engine needs, but in reality they are not flowing the whole valve. If they could give the engine the right amount of air that it needs and flow all of the valve, they can make the valve smaller. Next, you have to size the port to the valve size. Now everything in that port is very active. Velocity is up and atomization occurs at a lower RPM.

That's where a properly designed engine will respond better. It accelerates fast, takes off fast. You will usually get slightly better top end numbers, but the big gains in the port I just described are in the way it accelerates and runs at lower RPM. A smaller port with more velocity is the key.

What I just explained applies only to street bikes. When we do a race engine, we go all out. We say: what do we need in terms of horsepower to get it down the track within the rpm range of the bike, say 8000 RPM? You don't have to accelerate from a stop light with a passenger. You don't need as much bottom end.

When you design a head, ports in particular, can you lay out that process, step by step:

1. We have to define the engine size and parameters.

2. Then we decide what size hole we need to feed that engine, and also keep fuel atomized at low rpm. So we define the valve size that we need.

3. Then we design the intake port to be able to feed that amount of air. There are always corrections as we go through the process. Say it's a two-inch valve. We work backwards. We have formulas. We place the choke point far enough away from the valve to ensure that when the valve opens there's enough volume between the valve and the choke point that we are pulling in a good gulp of air and fuel. A cup's worth, not a shot glass worth. So the choke point is crucial in sizing and shape, and where it's placed.

Can you talk about the flow bench, what it does and where people go wrong in using the bench?

Most people with a flow bench fool themselves. I don't care how big or small a doorway is, if a guy is walking slow (because the valve is too big an the port is too big and the air is moving slow) he can walk through that door and take a

When Senior is found in the shop, it's usually in the "back room" attending to one of the CNC machines.

Note how each R&R head design has a matching piston - with a distinct squish zone.

hard right turn and hug the wall. Likewise, a too big valve and port being tested on a flow bench that doesn't move enough air will appear to flow all the valve. Now, back to the guy running, if I tell that guy to run through the door and turn hard he's going to overshoot. He basically shrinks the port because he's not flowing in the area where he's overshooting and it will form an eddy there and create turbulence in the port.

When you put the head on a flow bench that can't pull a lot of depression or create enough velocity, you won't see that overage - where the guy couldn't hug the corner. We've corrected our flow bench, modified our motor so we can move more air. Now we can pull over 100 inches of depression. So when we flow a head, we pull a huge depression to create a lot of velocity. And we have pitot tubes in the head and the cylinder. Then we know exactly what to correct.

However, if I flow that same head at 25 or 28 inches of depression, that's not enough to create the velocity necessary to point out the flaws in the port. It's easy to fool yourself, you're thinking

you're getting all the air around that valve, but you haven't because you haven't created the turbulence that will happen in the real world. In the real world, the piston on the intake stroke can pull close to 150 inches of depression when the crank is at 90 degrees and the piston is moving really fast.

We bought a flow bench and modified the hell out of it to be able to pull that huge velocity. Thus, we can see the turbulence in the port, the eddies. We also have a Super Flow 1050 that we use when we're dealing with carburetors, and a Super Flow 600.

So a flow bench is like a wind tunnel in reverse?

Yes it is, but again if the air in the tunnel is slow, if the air is only going 20 mph, what are you going to see? You can't see what's happening in the real world unless you speed up the air in the wind tunnel. Likewise, in the real world the engine is not working at 25 inches of depression, it's closer to 150 inches of depression. The closer you get up to that 150 figure on the bench, the more you learn about what's happening in the real world.

We've talked about ports and valves. Can we talk about the combustion chamber and what makes a good combustion chamber, and what makes a not-so-good combustion chamber?

We design the ports and the combustion chamber differently for different parts of the country. As an example, for riders in Arizona, I speed up the airflow through the head. So the air moves faster for complete combustion and less heat. In the Northeast we don't worry about that too much. We place little bumps in the combustion chamber so the air coming in dances a little around the exhaust valve. We want the air to warm up before ignition. Up here the air is cooler, the gas sits in the tank and it's cool.

Generally a bike runs better in cool air, the air molecules are packed together more densely. You're packing more air into the cylinder on each intake stroke. But when you pre-heat the charge in the head and combustion chamber before ignition; the combustion will be faster, and stronger.

Can you talk about squish, and the importance of squish?

It is extra important, especially in an engine that has too big a valve or too big a port. As the air-fuel comes in, the flat manufactured into the piston top comes up very close to the cylinder head - which squishes the air-fuel between the two surfaces, creating turbulence in the combustion chamber. That turbulence helps to atomize the fuel.

We put different size squish in different engines. With our billet engines, the bigger ones, 147 and 155 cubic inch motors, we want those heads to squish through the spark plug and create a faster, more complete, burn.

In an engine with domed pistons, we create squish on either side of the dome. We design them to compliment each other. One moves the charge through the spark plug, the other moves it toward the intake valve, it creates a swirl in the combustion chamber.

Final Comments?

When you're designing an engine or an intake port, you need a target you are designing toward.

With Jody Perewitz' Bonneville bike we had one

chance to design it and get it right. So, we worked backwards. We asked; what would be the air mass she had to push through, how much does the bike weigh, what is the coefficient of drag?

Then we could calculate how much torque we would need. Not horsepower, but torque, to get the job done. Then we had to design a relatively small engine that would put out that much torque. It was only a 100 cu in engine. Our goal was 200 mph with a relatively small engine.

Jody's bike is what I call a properly designed package. It was a team effort, of course. Danny Thayer, of three-stage oil pump fame, was their crew chief, he dialed it in on the salt. The point however, is that we had one shot to make it happen and we had to be able to determine what those "real world" conditions were, set the target, and design the engine to those conditions, that target.

With a lot of input from Senior, R&R is able to design, manufacture and balance their flywheel assemblies, which helps to explain why the 'wheels are both durable and smooth running.

Chapter Eight

Camchest

Cast off your Chains

As delivered from Harley-Davidson the Twin Cam engines feature two chains in the camchest. One to drive the rear-most cam, and a second chain that transfers that motion to the front camshaft.

From the very start the Twin Cams suffered issues with the chains and related tensioners. In typical American motorhead fashion, it wasn't long before the aftermarket brought out a solution - gear-drive cams.

Free yourself from those chains, said companies like S&S and Andrews. In place of the chains the aftermarket companies used two gears to connect the pinion shaft to the rear-most cam, and another set of gears - one on each cam - to transfer that energy to the second cam.

A lot of high performance V-Twins are assembled with gear drive cams in place of chains, and this R&R 124 inch engine is no different. All the components seen here are from S&S, except the support plate, which is a R&R component.

The assembly seen here is a gear drive installation on a R&R 124 cubic inch Twin Cam. The parts Jon is using are all from S&S, except the plate. The cam plate is R&R's own.

The assembly itself starts with the installation of the new Torrington bearings in the back of the camchest (in place of the stock INA bearings used by Milwaukee). Next, Jon applies abundant lubricant onto the outer end of the cams and then slides them both into the support plate. Yes, the two cams do need to be timed, as shown in the nearby photos. (Note, there's a similar sequence performed on a Harley-Davidson engine, as part of the assembly in chapter three.)

And because this is a gear-drive installation, there are two hydraulic ports - used to supply oil pressure to the newer hydraulic chain tensioners - that need to be closed off with the small plates supplied with the gear drive kit.

Before the plate and cams can be installed, however, the oil pump needs to be slipped in place on the pinion shaft. Installing the oil pump, and then the cam plate, requires the correct placement of three O-rings, as shown in the photo sequence. The plate itself is held in place with six Allen fasteners, the length of which differs depending on whether you're putting in an H-D or R&R cam plate.

There are four additional, and longer, Allen bolts that you need to hold the oil pump in place. "I like to tighten those gradually." explains Jon." "And I turn the engine over as I tighten them, so the pump can center itself as I snug up those bolts."

Next comes installation of the two timing gears. Jon warns that sometimes the gears have to be drawn onto the shafts, after doing a little TLC to the threads in the rear cam, and the holes in the gears where they mate with the shafts.

Finally it's time to drop the lifters into their bores, after a little pre-lubing. Care needs to be taken that the oil hole is oriented the right way and that the two small shafts that prevent the lifters from turning, are put in place.

Then it's just a matter of installing the lifter covers and the camchest cover.

1. The assembly of the cams and related components starts with installation of the Torrington bearings used in place of the factory's INA bearings.

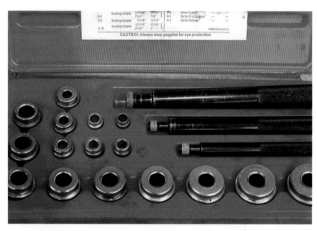

2. An installation kit comes with the correct driver...

3. ... for these particular bearings.

1. Jon drives the second inner bearing in until it comes up against the inner shoulder.

3. Both the drive gears and the cams (with their integral gears) are available in slightly smaller and larger sizes if the fitment turns out to be too tight or too loose.

2. With both inner bearings installed it's time to move on to the cams and support plate.

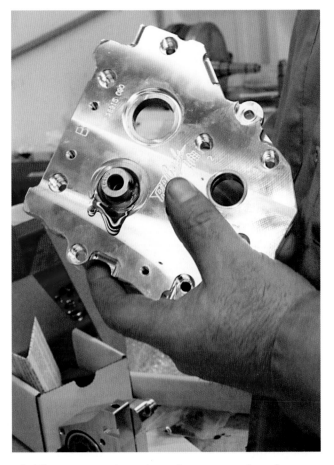

4. The rear cam is set into the support plate first...

1. Note the abundant use of assembly lube throughout this process.

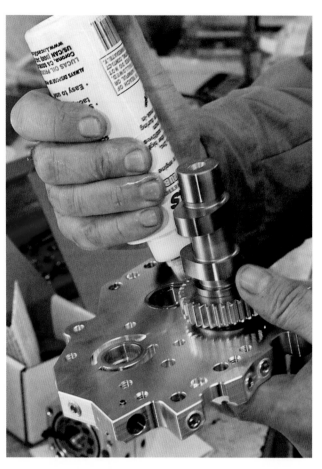

2. Jon lubes the bushing in the support plate before...

3. ... slipping the second cam into place.

4. Yes, the two cams do need to be timed - as shown. Jon puts a tie-wrap around the two cams so they can't jump a tooth, and then cuts it just before final installation of the cams and plate.

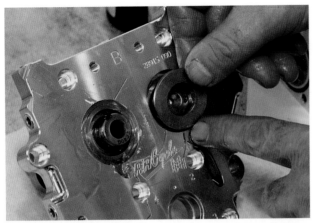

1. Once the 2 cams are installed correctly, Jon puts the spacer on the front cam...

2. ... followed by the snap ring...

4. To ensure the snap ring is fully seated in the groove.

3. ... and a little nudge from a screw driver...

5. Because this engine uses gear-drive cams, it's necessary to block off two oil ports in the support plate with the small covers seen here.

128

1. The smaller of the two block-off plates goes on first. If you look hard you can see the tie wrap used to keep the cams in time during the pre-assembly stage. The second block-off plate is installed near the end of the camchest assembly.

3. This O-ring seals the evacuation connection on the oil pump that draws oil from the crankcase - that connection is the bore seen right behind the O-ring.

2. Used out of sequence, this image is used to show the location of the upper block-off plate.

5. The 3-stage oil pump from Dan Thayer, the pump of choice at R&R.

Oil Pumps Dissected

When we think about the oil pump in our Twin Cam engines, we typically imagine it delivering pressurized oil to the crank, the cooing jets, the lifters and all the rest. There's another side of the oil pump, however, the suction side. The side responsible for evacuating the oil out of the engine cases and delivering it to the oil tank.

The pump just described would be called a two-stage pump: one for pressure and one for suction. Of late, more and more engine builders are paying more and more attention to the suction side of the oil pumps they put in their high performance V-Twin engines.

Eliminating as much oil as possible from the bottom end of your trusty Twin Cam means there's less oil in the blender being turned to a aerated froth by the churning flywheels. If there's less oil in the crankcase, then there's also less oil to slow the progress of the flywheels. At R&R, they like to use a three-stage pump, specifically the pump manufactured by Dan Thayer.

Machined from 6061 aluminum, Dan's pump is a true three-stage design, with two suction "sides," one to evacuate the flywheel cavity and one to pull the oil from the camchest. This pump is also designed to cycle extra oil picked up on the suction side back to the oil tank where the air and oil can separate, instead of to the pressure side where aerated oil can raise havoc with the lifters.

With Twin Cam engines, it's hard to talk about the oil pump without also talking about the cam support plate. The plate not only supports the outer end of the camshafts, it also regulates the oil pressure and acts as the distributor of oil leaving the pump.

The R&R support plate is cut in-house from billet aluminum.

The three-stage oil pump from Dan Thayer contains 3 separate gerotor sets - each cut from billet aluminum - two for scavenging and one for pressure.

Oil Pumps Dissected

The more typical OEM-style pump is a two-stage affair, with 2 separate gerotors - one for suction and one for pressure.

The strength of the billet combined with precision machining means a support plate that does an excellent job of both supporting the cams, and distributing the flow of oil.

Available in three models, depending on the year of the engine and whether it uses gear or chain drive the plate will work with either the Dan Thayer pump, or an OEM style two-stage pump.

It's important to note that not all pumps play well with all support plates. So when you're making a decision on which oil pump to run, be sure to use a cam support plate that works with your pump and style of cam drive.

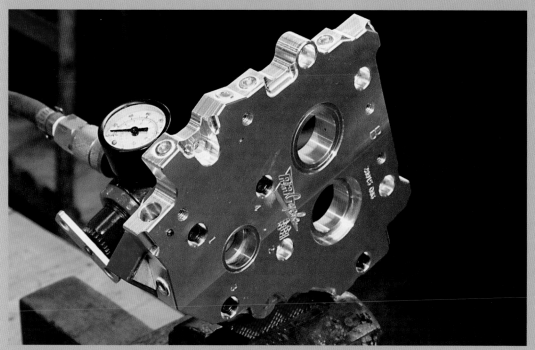

A quality support plate is important for multiple reasons. Not only does it support and help locate the camshafts, it also controls the oil pressure.

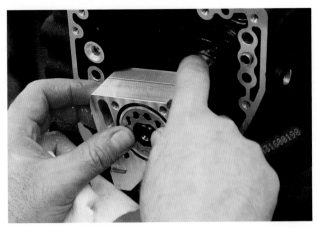

1. Assembly time, starting with the pre-lubed 3-stage oil pump.

4. ... Time now to cut the tie-wrap and install the cams and support plate.

2. Next, the two O-rings mentioned in an earlier caption.

3. A squirt of pre-lube on the pinion shaft...

5. Jon slides the assembly into place slow and easy.

1. The plate in place, waiting for the 6 fasteners that bolt it securely in place

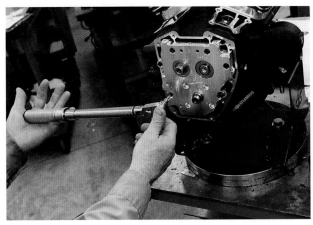

3. The fasteners are tightened to 10 to 12 ft. lbs.

4. Four relatively long and equal-length fasteners are used to secure the oil pump to the support plate - regardless of the brand of plate or oil pump.

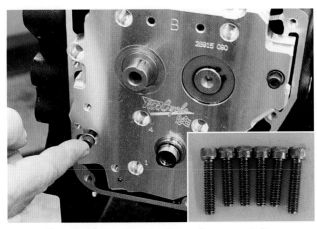

2. With an R&R support plate, there are 2 longer bolts and 4 shorter. In the case of an H-D plate, 2 of the holes are counter bored so all 6 fasteners are the same length.

5. Jon rotates the crank as he tightens these 4 bolts... so he knows nothing is binding, and that the oil pump has a chance to center itself. Final torque is the same as the other 6 - 10 to 12 ft. lbs. .

1. The 2 drive gears, the lower one in particular, don't always want to slide onto their respective shafts - so a little oil, and dressing of the gear's I.D. with a small file, are often in order.

2. Once again, installing the 2 gears means...

3. ... paying attention to the timing marks on the gears. Before screwing in the 2 bolts that hold the gears to their shafts, it's also a good idea to chase the threads in the pinion shaft and rear cam, (then clean the threads and add Loctite).

4. The specification for the upper gear is 30, for the lower it's 20 ft. lbs. Use blue Loctite on the (cleaned) threads.

5. Here's the install of the last block-off plate.

1. The new lifters are from S&S...

3. Jon drops the lifters in with the oil hole in the lifter facing the cam support plate - the source of the oil.

2. It's a good idea to work some oil down into those needle bearings before installation.

4. Don't forget the small pin which prevents the lifter from rotating.

Chapter Nine

The Dyno

More than just Bragging Rights

We all know about Dynos, and anyone who's had their bike on a dyno knows the importance of those final numbers for horsepower and torque - and the sense of satisfaction we feel when the dyno run nets good numbers - numbers we can brag about at the local watering hole.

In reality the Dyno is one more tool available to mechanics and techs lucky enough to have access to what can be used for everything from setting up an engine before it leaves the

A dyno is a very useful tool. Good for finding runability issues as well as tuning an engine for maximum output. Ultimately the success or failure of a dyno depends not on the dyno but on the person running the dyno.

shop after serious engine work, to massaging the last ounce of power from a new or old V-twin, or metric four-banger if that's your preference.

Seen in the nearby photos is Brandon with a fresh 103 equipped with R&R's Stage 4 kit. "I don't like to do full pulls on a fresh engine," explains Brandon. "The bottom end isn't the problem, the problem is the cylinder and rings. Those rings are sharp, and when you accelerate hard you are pushing that edge right up against the cross-hatch that the engine guy so carefully cut into those cylinders. It's like taking a razor blade to that cross-hatch."

In this case, Brandon has just installed a map in the Bagger's CPU, a map that he thinks is close to correct based on his experience with similar late model 103s equipped with the same Stage 4 kit. "You can take two identical engines, same year, equipment and all the rest," explains Brandon, "and develop a perfect map for the first one, put that same map in the second motorcycle, and it will need to be adjusted. So, even though the map I've installed worked great in a nearly identical bike, the bike still needs to be run on the dyno. And because this bike has zero miles, I need to set it a little rich for break in. After he has 500 or 600 miles on the bike, I'll have him bring it back

Ultimately it's all about creating a map - a map that ensures the engine gets the right amount of fuel, and a spark at exactly the right instant, under nearly any running condition.

Data - the dyno delivers data by the electronic bucket full. It's up to the tech to interpret that data and find the conditions where the bike's ECU isn't doing an optimum job of managing the timing curve or fuel delivery.

and then we can do full-power pulls, and readjust the fuel and ignition curves for maximum power."

Each part-throttle pull generates a graph (actually a series of graphs if that's what the tech wants) as seen in one of the nearby photo boxes. Along the bottom is the fuel line, the line that indicates the air-fuel ratio at a certain RPM and load combinations. Brandon's job is to go into the map, the part of the map that controls the fuel under the same RPM and load, and richen the mixture where the line goes up above his ideal ratio and lean it out where the line dips down, which indicates a too-rich mixture.

With each part-throttle pull the resulting fuel line gets flatter and flatter.

Q and A with Brandon

How long have you been doing dyno runs and where did you get your training?

I've been doing this for thirteen years. The training was done in-house, I developed most of the tuning technics myself.

Tell me what a Dyno is?

I tell customers the dyno is a road that goes nowhere. It's a tool for monitoring and adjusting the way an engine runs under different loads and conditions. Although the main idea in peoples' minds is the horsepower and torque numbers, one could buy two identical dynos, run the same bike on the same day one after the other and the numbers will be different due to additional bearing drag from one dyno to

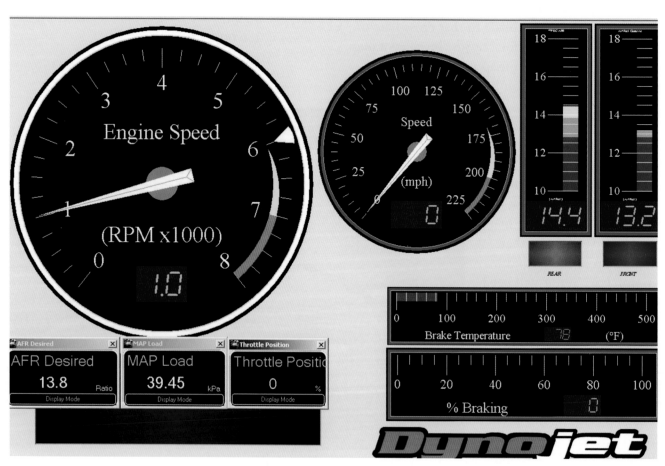

Dyno screen shot #1. This shows the dyno software in makerun mode to do the pulls and record the data.

another etc. In the end it's a safe controlled way to correct fuel and timing for optimum performance and economy for the fuel injected motorcycles. It's also a great tool for us in the shop to know if our performance packages and engines are doing what they are supposed to, as well as helping us develop new performance products and make sure those are headed in the right direction.

In a typical dyno run, what are your goals, what are you looking for?

When I begin tuning, the first thing I do is make it safe in terms of fuel and timing - then I make it fast. Most of the "pulls" are used to log air/fuel ratio over the rpm range. I perform series of pulls at a fixed throttle position (or manifold pressure on some models) based on

where the fuel adjustment is broken down in the fuel injection tuner. On carbureted engines my pulls are based on where different fuel circuits start and overlap. The idea is to get the fuel line on the graph straight throughout the pull at the target air / fuel ratio. Normally at wide open throttle I like to see it between 12.9-13.3 depending on the build. For steady state cruising at light throttle I like it to be around 14.2.

Once I know the fuel is happy then I begin timing adjustments. I do fuel first because it's safe - there will be no lean load conditions. Also, when you begin to advance your timing, if you do get some detonation (pinging), you know it's because the timing is too advanced and not because it's lean. Very often fuel adjustments are necessary again after timing has been

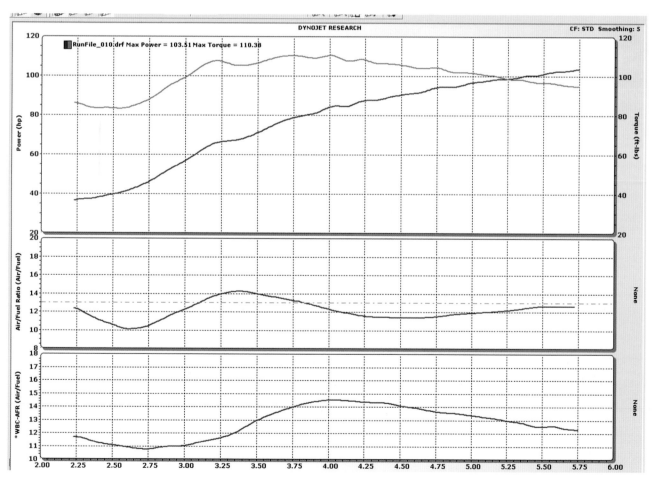

Screen shot #2. This typical dyno graphic shows the results of the pull in horsepower, torque and air fuel for both the front and rear cylinders.

properly set. Remember this, fuel will never affect timing, but timing can affect fuel.

So the dyno is not simply a tool to measure horsepower and torque?

Tuning for the best drivability and efficiency is by far the best attribute of a dyno. The Dyno can be used to diagnosing other issues, noises, vibration, and speedo calibrations. Measuring horsepower and torque are excellent by-products and used mainly when we are developing packages or products to make sure we are going in the right direction.

Am I correct, that really all you typically can do is check the air-fuel and ignition timing at various RPMS and load situations.

True, but with more advanced dyno setups

(4 gas sensors, torque gauges etc.) they can be used to develop exhaust systems, cam design for EPA certifications and much more. But for street and even race tuning the extras aren't needed. Many dynos have eddie-current braking systems to simulate mild to extreme loads both for diagnoses and stress testing as well as simulation of road conditions.

Can the results of one dyno be compared to another in a different location?

Yes and no. As I said before, no two dynos measure the same. Most of the time when I compare dynos I'm looking at the curves and their shape. Also, don't forget dyno graphs can be easily fudged.

Is it OK to do full-pull dyno runs on a new or just-rebuilt engine?

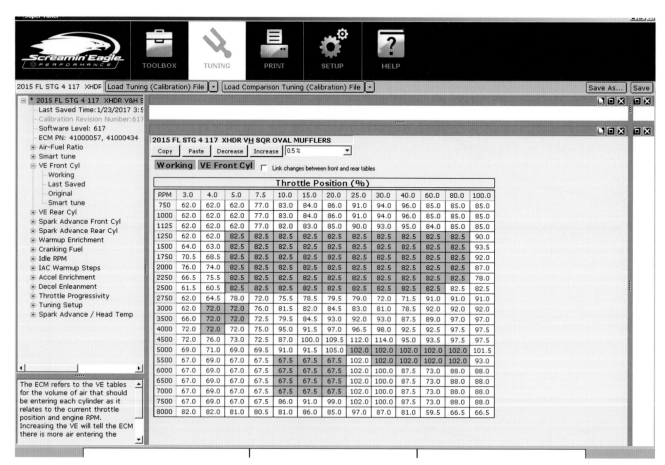

Screen shot #3. This shows Brandon adjusting the fuel tables in the particular tuner this bike has (Screaming Eagle Race Tuner in this case). Then applying the changes.

Not really. It will do it, but hard acceleration stress on fresh piston rings will cause excessive cylinder wear or damaged rings that will not seat properly. Also, as you ride your motorcycle and it gets hot and cold over and over it makes the components inside the engine harder and stronger, its like heat treating your engine. I tell customers to ride it civilized for 500-600 miles, (no lugging or over revving). It's the pistons' rate of change or acceleration that will drive the sharp edges of the rings into the cylinder wall. As the rings wear in during the first 500 miles or so they round off and mate themselves to the cylinder around them.

Over bloated numbers that they're either told or simply get into their minds are one of the biggest problems. Looking though catalogs or graphs viewed on the web tend to set the bar higher than you're likely to see in reality. Different exhaust choices or cams that were designed for a particular kit can impact performance and numbers greatly. But even if everything is built and setup right, improper tuning will bring numbers down and running quality down as well. Most of my tunes done during the summer riding months are retunes from other shops in the area or even several states away.

Why are so many people disappointed in the results of their dyno runs. What goes wrong?

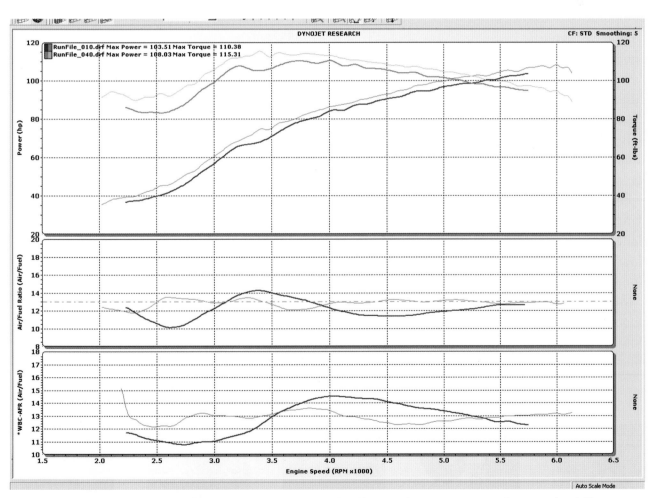

Dyno screen shot #4. This final shot shows the next set of pulls over the previous run, showing the difference not only in power but in the air-fuel coming out of the pipe. Ultimately it shows that optimum fuel ratio nets best power.

Books from Wolfgang Publications can be found at many book stores and numerous web sites.

Titles	ISBN	Price	# of pages
Advanced Airbrush Art	9781929133208	$27.95	144 pages
Advanced Custom Motorcycle Assembly & Fabrication	9781929133239	$27.95	144 pages
Advanced Custom Motorcycle Wiring - *Revised*	9781935828761	$27.95	144 pages
Advanced Pinstripe Art	9781929133321	$27.95	144 pages
Advanced Sheet Metal Fab	9781929133123	$27.95	144 pages
Advanced Tattoo Art - *Revised*	9781929133822	$27.95	144 pages
Airbrush How-To with Mickey Harris	9781929133505	$27.95	144 pages
Building Hot Rods	9781929133437	$27.95	144 pages
Colorful World of Tattoo Models	9781935828716	$34.95	144 pages
Composite Materials 1	9781929133765	$27.95	144 pages
Composite Materials 2	9781929133932	$27.95	144 pages
Composite Materials 3	9781935828662	$27.95	144 pages
Composite Materials Step by Step Projects	9781929133369	$27.95	144 pages
Cultura Tattoo Sketchbook	9781935828839	$32.95	284 pages
Custom Bike Building Basics	9781935828624	$24.95	144 pages
Custom Motorcycle Fabrication	9781935828792	$27.95	144 pages
Harley-Davidson Sportster Hop-Up & Customizing Guide	9781935828952	$27.95	144 pages
Harley-Davidson Sportser Buell Engine Hop-Up Guide	9781929133093	$24.95	144 pages
Harley-Davidson Twin Cam-Hop Up	9781929133697	29.95	144 pages
Harley-Davidson Evo Hop-Up/Build	9781941064337	29.95	144 pages
How Airbrushes Work	9781929133710	$24.95	144 pages
Honda Enthusiast Guide Motorcycles 1959-1985	9781935828853	$27.95	144 pages
Honda Mini Trail	9781941064320	29.95	144 pages
How-To Airbrush, Pinstripe & Goldleaf	9781935828693	$27.95	144 pages
How-To Build Old Skool Bobber - 2nd Edition	9781935828785	$27.95	144 pages

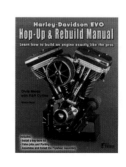

Books from Wolfgang Publications can be found at many book stores and numerous web sites.

Titles	ISBN	Price	# of pages
How-To Build a Cheap Chopper	9781929133178	$27.95	144 pages
How-To Build Cafe Racer	9781935828730	$27.95	144 pages
How-To Chop Tops	9781929133499	$24.95	144 pages
How-To Fix American V-Twin	9781929133727	$27.95	144 pages
How-To Paint Tractors & Trucks	9781929133475	$27.95	144 pages
Hot Rod Wiring	9781929133987	$27.95	144 pages
Hot Rod Chassis How-To	9781929133703	$29.95	144 Pages
Kosmoski's *New* Kustom Paint Secrets	9781929133833	$27.95	144 pages
Learning the English Wheel	9781935828891	$27.95	144 pages
Mini Ebooks - Butterfly and Roses	9781935828167	Ebook Only	
Mini Ebooks - Skulls & Hearts	9781935828198	Ebook Only	
Mini Ebooks - Lettering & Banners	9781935828204	Ebook Only	
Mini Ebooks - Tribal Stars	9781935828211	Ebook Only	
Power Hammers	9781929133604	29.95	144 pages
Pro Pinstripe	9781929133925	$27.95	144 pages
Sheet Metal Bible	9781929133901	$29.95	176 pages
Sheet Metal Fab Basics B&W	9781929133468	$24.95	144 pages
Sheet Metal Fab for Car Builders	9781929133383	$27.95	144 pages
SO-CAL Speed Shop, Hot Rod Chassis	9781935828860	$27.95	144 pages
Tattoo Bible #1	9781929133840	$27.95	144 pages
Tattoo Bible #2	9781929133857	$27.95	144 pages
Tattoo Bible #3	9781935828754	$27.95	144 pages
Tattoo Lettering Bible	9781935828921	$27.95	144 pages
Tattoo Sketchbook, Jim Watson	9781935828037	$32.95	112 pages
Triumph Restoration - Pre Unit	9781929133635	$29.95	144 pages
Triumph Restoration - Unit 650cc	9781929133420	$29.95	144 pages
Vintage Dirt Bikes - Enthusiast's Guide	9781929133314	$27.95	144 pages
Ultimate Sheet Metal Fab	9780964135895	$24.95	144 pages
Ultimate Triumph Collection	9781935828655	$49.95	144 pages

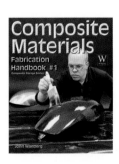
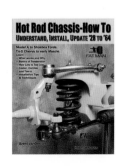

Notes